Welcome to Spain

R. A. N. Dixon

Collins
Glasgow and London

Cover photographs
Peter Baker, Van Phillips, Bill Stirling,
Syndication International

Photographs
J. Allan Cash Ltd
p 24 (rt), 44, 60, 94

Peter Baker
p 45

Van Phillips
p 39

Picturepoint Ltd
p 31

Bill Stirling
p 24 (top and bottom 1.), 36, 49, 79

ZEFA
p 29, 50, 69, 73

Regional maps
Matthews & Taylor Associates

Town plans
M. and R. Piggott

Illustrations
Barry Rowe

First published 1980
Revised edition 1985
Copyright © R. A. N. Dixon 1980
Published by William Collins Sons and Company Limited
Printed in Great Britain
ISBN 0 00 447396 5

HOW TO USE THIS BOOK

The contents page of this book shows how the country is divided up into autonomous regions. The book is in two sections: general information and gazetteer. The latter is arranged by regions with an introduction and a map (detail below left). There are also plans of the main towns (detail below right). All the towns and villages in the gazetteer are shown on the maps. Places to visit and leisure facilities available in each region and town are indicated by symbols. Main roads, railways, ferries and airports are shown on the maps and plans.

Regional Maps

Symbol	Meaning	Symbol	Meaning
✝	religious building	🏃	waterskiing
🏛	museum or gallery	⛵	sailing
🏰	castle	🤿	diving
🏤	notable building	🌳	deciduous forest
m	ancient monument	🌲	evergreen forest
❋	park	☐	natural reserve
🐘	zoo		
⛰	spa		
✈	airport		
✦	aerodrome		
▲	mountaineering		
caves			
⛷	skiing		

metres	feet
2000	6561
1000	3281
400	1312
200	656
0	0

Scale 1 : 2,500,000

```
0    20   40   60   80 kms
0  10  20  30  40  50 miles
```

Town Maps

Symbol	Meaning	Symbol	Meaning
✝	religious building	❋	garden
🏛	museum or gallery	🌳	park
🏰	castle	🐘	zoo
🏤	notable building	●	railway station
m	ancient monument	🚌	bus station
POL	police	✈	airport
✉	post office	✦	aerodrome
i	tourist information	🏃	stadium
⚒	town hall	≈	swimming pool
📖	library	🏇	racecourse
➕	hospital	T	telephone office
▣	theatre	⚓	harbour
✺	casino	⛱	beach
🏠	market		
▲	youth hostel		

Every effort has been made to give you an up-to-date text but changes are constantly occurring and we will be grateful for any information about changes you may notice while travelling.

CONTENTS

Town Plans

Regions and Provinces

Galicia (Galiza)
1 La Coruña 2 Lugo
3 Pontevedra 4 Orense

Asturias
5 Asturias

Castilla y León
 6 León
 7 Palencia
 8 Burgos
 9 Zamora
10 Valladolid
11 Soria
12 Salamanca
13 Ávila
14 Segovia

Cantabria
15 Cantabria

La Rioja
16 La Rioja

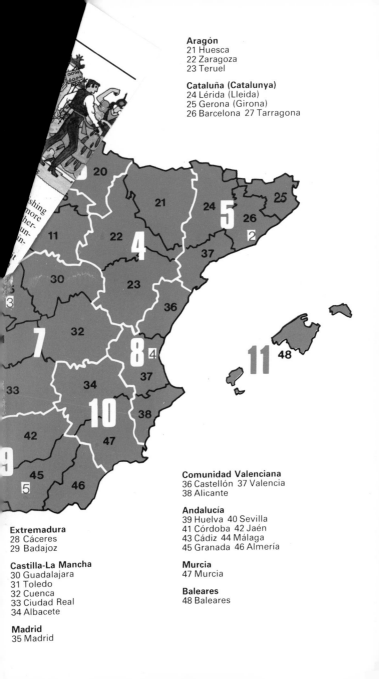

Aragón
21 Huesca
22 Zaragoza
23 Teruel

Cataluña (Catalunya)
24 Lérida (Lleida)
25 Gerona (Girona)
26 Barcelona 27 Tarragona

Comunidad Valenciana
36 Castellón 37 Valencia
38 Alicante

Andalucía
39 Huelva 40 Sevilla
41 Córdoba 42 Jaén
43 Cádiz 44 Málaga
45 Granada 46 Almería

Murcia
47 Murcia

Baleares
48 Baleares

Extremadura
28 Cáceres
29 Badajoz

Castilla-La Mancha
30 Guadalajara
31 Toledo
32 Cuenca
33 Ciudad Real
34 Albacete

Madrid
35 Madrid

SPAIN

Spain (*España*) can be said to lie between two continents – Europe and Africa – and between two seas – the Mediterranean and the Atlantic. It comprises five-sixths of the Iberian Peninsula which it shares with Portugal and with the tiny British colony of Gibraltar.

To the north it has the massive mountain border of the Pyrenees, 677km/421mi long, separating it from France and from the principality of Andorra. To the west, its border with Portugal is half as long again. To the south, only 13km/8mi away across the straits and clearly visible, lies Africa. In Peninsular Spain there are 47 provinces and these provinces are grouped into 15 regions. There are also the Balearic Islands which are administratively grouped into a single province, which is also a region.

Spain is the largest country in Europe after Russia and France. It is twice the size of the whole United Kingdom but only one-twentieth the size of the United States, hardly bigger, in fact, than the state of California.

It has some of the highest and loveliest mountains in Europe. The Sierra Nevada, in the south, with its peak of Mulhacén (3480m/11,417ft) is snow-capped all the year round, as are parts of the Pyrenees. In the centre are the Guadarramas, in the north bordering the Bay of Biscay, the Picos de Europa.

Spain's four main rivers, which bring fertility to its largely sun-dried lands, are the Tajo, or Tagus (910km/565mi), the Ebro (928km/577mi), the Duero (770 km/478mi) and the Guadalquivir (560km/348mi). Its four main cities are its capital Madrid (pop. 3,188,300), Barcelona (1,755,000), Valencia (751,700) and Sevilla (653,800). Between them they account for nearly one-fifth of Spain's total population of 36,000,000.

Even without the Balearic Islands, Spain has 3000km/1864mi of coastline. Sixty percent of it is rocky, often breathtakingly beautiful, but unsuitable for bathing. But that still leaves 1000km/621mi of mostly sandy beaches. Half the coastline is washed by the warm and tideless Mediterranean, the rest by an Atlantic more benevolent than it is to countries further north. Indeed, Spain's Atlantic coast, from Gibraltar up to Portugal, is even warmer in winter than that of the Mediterranean. On the whole of Spain's seaboard there is really no winter. Snow, if it falls at all, melts and disappears in half an hour. Occasionally there is frost but only at night. Even in the north, on the Biscay coast, the flour of such shrubs as bougainvillaea is indicative of mild winters than any mometer – as the greenness of the co tryside is more eloquent than any ra gauge.

The beaches of Spain help to make the most popular holiday country i Europe and are, of course, its fortune Without tourism the books would neve balance, for Spain buys abroad more goods than she sells. Each year the number of tourists who visit the country exceeds the entire population who live there. Nevertheless Spain is the world' tenth most important industrial nation the fifth largest in shipbuilding and fourth in the production of wine. It produce more olive oil than any other country and is also the world's largest exporter o apricots and of building cement. Even the mercury in your thermometer is likely to have come from Spain. Nowadays Spain manufactures and exports large numbers of motorcars – of Italian, French, Amer ican and British design – but has begun to import more and more cars from other countries. The country has a few oil wells but none of any importance.

For the sightseer Spain has everything. It has art, architecture and the relics of more than 2000 years of history and culture. There are castles, bridges, aqueducts, roads and amphitheatres buil by the Romans during the 200 years before the birth of Christ and the 400 years after. There are palaces, fountains, mosques, public baths and more castles (mostly square ones) built by the Moors who ruled Spain for even longer than the Romans did. There are cathedrals, chur ches, monasteries, sanctuaries, paintings, sculptures – and of course more castles (mostly round ones) – dating from Spain's Golden Age when for a brief 100 years her mighty empire comprised most of South and Central America, Cuba, the West Indies, the Low Countries, parts of France and Italy, Portugal and large slices of Africa.

There are still primitive villages where the farmer and his cows and chickens live in the same building, where corn is threshed with the flail, the land ploughed by mules or even cows, the produce taken to market in pannier bags on the backs of donkeys, where women wash clothes in the streams and carry them home in baskets on their heads.

Nevertheless Spain – especially around the coasts and in the tourist areas – is in many ways a modern country. Her hotels are the most modern in Europe – a surprising thing until one remembers that they have nearly all been built since the massive tourist boom started around 1950. It also has modern motorways, holiday resorts, airports, football stadiums, camping sites and shops and there are few places, even quite small villages, without a night club or a discotheque.

As Spain is such a large country, and has so diverse a history and so varied a climate, it is natural that there are appreciable differences of character, dialect, dress and housing between the people of its various regions. Some of these differences are summed up by the Spaniards themselves when they say that the Catalan saves, the Andalusian sings, the Basque acts, the Castilian dreams, the Extremaduran fights and the Galician yearns for what is not to be.

But the Spaniard, no matter where he comes from, has one basic characteristic. He is the most generous and helpful person in the world and the most hospitable to the foreigner. People who have been to Spain before will know this. Those who have not will discover it in half an hour. You begin to feel this hospitality the moment you set foot in the country and you are overwhelmed with it at a time of illness or need or misfortune. If you ask the way in other countries you will usually be told, but you may be made to feel that you are delaying an important appointment. A Spaniard will go with you and show you, even if the place you want is on the other side of town.

Spaniards have a natural courtesy. They never enter a shop without a greeting. As they pass your table in a restaurant they wish you *¡que aproveche!* the Spanish equivalent of *bon appétit* (to which the correct answer is merely *gracias*, thank you). In a railway carriage they will politely offer their food to you first before starting to eat it themselves, an offer it is customary to decline equally politely. When you visit Spanish friends for the first time they will tell you: *Es su casa*, this is your house, a charming welcome that has of course no legal validity.

Spaniards talk with their hands, even into a telephone. They always talk in loud voices, so that the friendliest of discussions has all the appearance to foreigners of a first-class row. They have a great sense of humour. They are individualists. They treat authority – and one-way streets – with scorn. Their drink is wine, even at breakfast, even in prison, but they seldom drink it to excess. They love noise and crowds. They care for old people and worship children.

They have a dignity and an equality and an absence of servility which wealth, poverty or position does not alter. This applies equally to the warm, two-handed handshake of the king, to the shoeshine boy talking to you of Beethoven, and to the old Aragonese shepherd who took part in a demonstration of the *jota* for Prince Bernhard who was visiting the Dutch Embassy in Madrid. When the prince shook hands with him afterwards the old shepherd said: 'If ever you find yourself in Teruel *Vd. sabe dónde tiene su casa*, you know where you have your house.'

Spanish virtues – as well as Spanish faults – come straight from the heart, where all genuine things come from. The Spanish heart is not only in the right place, it is several sizes bigger than normal, and twice as warm. From it flows *simpatía*, a word for which there is no equivalent in the English language but which means the sort of innate kindness and friendliness that makes one remember one's stay in their country with nostalgia and be determined to return.

THE ARTS

Painting

Spain's first painter of importance, whose life spanned three-quarters of its 'golden century', was **Luis Morales** (1509-86). Born at Badajoz, fervent portrayer of realistic religious subjects, he was asked to contribute to the adornment of the palace-monastery at El Escorial but his *Christ and the Cross* failed to please Philip II and it went instead to St Jerome's Church, Madrid.

El Greco, 'the Greek' (1541-1614), whose real name was Domenico Theotocopuli and who was Spanish only by adoption, was similarly unsuccessful with Philip II and his *Martyrdom of St Maurice* was stored away unseen. El Greco studied under Titian and Tintoretto in Venice and after eight years in Rome went to Spain at the age of 34 (see **Toledo**). His elongated human figures, which have led some people to suggest that he suffered from astigmatism, are masterpieces that have seldom been surpassed.

Ribalta (1551-1628) and **Ribera** (1588-1656) were both born in the region of Valencia. Ribalta, who had two artist sons, painted religious subjects. He studied in Rome, returned to Valencia and had Ribera as one of his pupils. Ribera, on the other hand, went to Italy and stayed there, becoming known as *Lo Spagnoletto*, 'the little Spaniard'. His output of both oils and engravings was enormous. Nevertheless he died poor, also feeling ashamed of his daughter's love affair with John Joseph of Austria.

Zurbarán (1598-1664), born at Badajoz, son of a labourer, worked for nearly all the convents and religious houses of Spain. His praying and meditating friars are typical examples of his genius.

Spain's greatest painter and one of the greatest painters of all time, **Velázquez** (1599-1660), born at Sevilla, was able, it has been said, to portray empty space and make it real. At 24 he took to Madrid a specimen of his work (the famous street scene, the *Water Seller*, later presented by Ferdinand VII to the Duke of Wellington) and was commissioned by Philip IV to paint his portrait (the first of 40 he did of this monarch) and appointed court painter. His studio was in the palace and the king spent much time watching him work. Having made friends with Rubens in Madrid, Velázquez painted *Los Borrachos* (The Drunkards) to pay for a journey to Italy to see him. His work was little known outside court circles until 1818 when the royal collection became the nucleus of the Prado Museum.

A fellow Andalusian and contemporary **Alonso Cano** (1601-67), though brilliant in painting, sculpture and architecture, was a man of turbulent character. He fled his native Granada after a duel, left Madrid when the crown prince, whom he was coaching, complained of his rudeness, was accused of murdering his wife but freed after a spell on the rack had failed to produce a confession, trained as a priest until his unbearable temper became too much for his superiors and finally, on his

death bed, after refusing a proffered crucifix because it was amateurishly carved, demanded a simple cross of sticks fastened with cord.

Murillo (1617-82), famous for his Virgins and saints, was born in Sevilla, orphaned at ten, brought up by an uncle, had nine children most of whom became priests or nuns, refused Charles II's invitation to Madrid and fell to his death from a scaffolding while painting a mural in a Cádiz church.

The great, versatile and hot-tempered **Goya** (1746-1828), painter of superb portraits, Napoleonic atrocities, cartoons, the two famous *majas*, bullfighting scenes, and the witches, monsters and goblins of his 'black period', was born at Fuentetodos (Zaragoza), went completely deaf at 60 and died at 82.

After Goya there is a long gap until the births of **Zuloaga** (1870-1945), the Basque who painted portraits and bullfight scenes and gained fame in Britain and the USA; the Catalan **Sert** (1876-1945) who painted murals in Paris, Geneva, London and New York as well as Spain (see **Vic**) and married Princess Mdivani; **Picasso** (1881-1973), born in Málaga but who spent his teens (his 'blue period') in Barcelona and the rest of his long life in France, never returning to Spain because of his disapproval of Franco; **Salvador Dalí** (b. 1905) the eccentric, extrovert, surrealist painter and jewelry designer; and **Joan Miró** (1895-1983), another member of the surrealist group, who designed the murals for the UNESCO building in Paris and the airport building at Barcelona.

Music

Spain has produced four internationally-known composers, all born within about 30 years of each other. **Sarasate** (1844-1908) of Pamplona, son of a military bandsman, played the violin at three, gave his first concert at seven and became orphaned and required to fend for himself at 12 on the death from cholera of his mother in France. At 23 he won first prize at the Paris Conservatoire and became the most famous virtuoso of his time. Queen Isabel II presented him with a Stradivarius violin and he later acquired another. He gave concerts in many countries including Britain, USA and Russia. Among his compositions: *Bohemian Airs, Jota Aragonesa, Zapateado*.

Albéniz (1860-1909), born at Camprodón (Girona), was also an infant prodigy. He gave his first piano concert (in Barcelona) at four, was studying in Paris (under Debussy and Liszt) at seven and touring Cuba and the Philippines at 12-14. In his twenties he was giving piano lessons in

Barcelona and married one of his pupils. In 1908 he received the Legion of Honour but contracted Bright's disease. His many works include the *Iberia* suite, *Tango* and several operas, two of them in English.

Granados (1867-1916), pianist and composer of many Spanish dances, seven operas and the famous *Goyescas* (inspired by Goya's pictures), was born at Lleida (Lérida). He went to New York in 1915 ready for the presentation at the Metropolitan Opera House of his opera based on *Goyescas*. Its performance on 26 January 1916 was a triumphal success. As he was on the point of returning to Spain, he received an invitation from President Wilson to visit the White House, cancelled his passage and embarked instead on the liner *Sussex* which was torpedoed in the Atlantic by a German submarine. Granados, with most of the passengers and crew, was drowned.

De Falla (1876-1946), born at Cádiz, composer of the melodious *Nights in the Gardens of Spain* for piano and orchestra, *The Three Cornered Hat*, a ballet which he wrote for Diaghilev, *Love, the Sorcerer*, which includes the famous *Fire Dance*, the opera *The Short Life* and much else, studied in Madrid and Paris (meeting Ravel, Debussy and Dukas) spent most of his life in Spain but went to Argentina during the Civil War (1936-9) and died there. His *Atlántida*, based on the epic poem by the Catalan poet Verdaguer (1845-1902), for solo, choir and orchestra, was first performed after his death.

The growing popularity of *Concierto de Aranjuez* for guitar and orchestra has brought fame to a fifth composer, **Joaquín** Rodrigo (b. 1902) a pupil of Dukas and blind from the age of three.

Literature

Of Spain's many outstanding writers spanning nearly nine centuries, from the philosophers **Averroes**, the Moslem (1126-98), and **Maimónides**, the Jew (1135-1204), both born at Córdoba at the height of its Moslem cultural influence, to **García Lorca** (1898-1936), Spain's Rupert Brooke, **Ortega y Gasset** (1883-1955) and the Nobel prize-winner **Benavente** (1866-1954), there is room here for only two.

Cervantes (1547-1616), by far the greatest of all Spanish writers (see **Alcalá de Henares**), was 58 on publication of the first part of *Don Quixote* and 69 on that of the second part. He had previously written many other works – short novels (also of outstanding merit), *La Galatea*, a pastoral romance, about 30 plays, only two of which have survived, and a poem of 3000 lines. He was wounded in the battle of Lepanto, imprisoned by the corsairs in Algiers, ransomed after four daring attempts to escape and afterwards imprisoned for debt at Sevilla.

His contemporary **Lope de Vega** (1562-1635), who wrote sneeringly of *Don Quixote*, is said to have been the most prolific writer of all time. He wrote 1500 plays (his first at the age of 12), 400 *autos*, or religious pieces, an exultant poem for the death of the British admiral Drake and another on Mary Stuart and still had time to beget six children (three of them illegitimate), become a priest and sail in the Spanish Armada (still scribbling away on the voyage).

CURRENCY

The Spanish unit of currency is the *peseta* (pta) which is sub-divided into 100 *céntimos*. There are notes for 5000, 2000, 1000, 500, 200 and 100 ptas and coins for 100, 50, 25, 10, 5 and 1 ptas.

Foreign currency notes and travellers' cheques can be changed without formality, other than the production of one's passport, at banks and travel agencies (most of which prominently display a list of the ruling exchange rates) and at better-class hotels. The exchange rate is always better for travellers' cheques than for notes. Spanish for change is *cambio*.

Banking hours Open 0900–1400 Monday to Saturday all the year except June to Sept. when Saturday 0900-1300.

HOW TO GET THERE

Plane There are regular air services from several towns in Britain to the main Spanish towns and tourist areas. The flying time London-Barcelona is two hours, Palma de Mallorca two and a quarter hours, Málaga two and a half hours. In addition there are numerous all-inclusive or 'package' holidays for various categories of hotel and lengths of stay. From the USA there are direct flights to Madrid and Barcelona.

Train British Rail, in conjunction with the French and Spanish railway companies, offer through services to most of the Spanish tourist areas: approximate overall travelling times from London: San Sebastián 18 hours, Barcelona 25 hours, Alicante 33 hours. Sleeping cars or couchettes are available on most services and cars can be transported from Boulogne as far as Narbonne or Biarritz.

Coach Several coach firms offer economical travel between London and Spain. Approximate overall travelling time, including Channel crossing and overnight stop in France: Barcelona 41½ hours, Benidorm 49½ hours, Marbella 65½ hours. On some journeys there is no overnight stop and these times are correspondingly reduced.

Boat There is at present only one service direct from Britain to Spain (Plymouth–Santander): crossing time approximately 24 hours. From New York it is possible to sail to Algeciras, Cádiz and Barcelona.

IF YOU ARE MOTORING

Documents The only documents required, apart fom a valid passport, are an international motor insurance certificate ('green card'), which is obtainable from the insurers of the vehicle, and an international driving permit, obtainable from any of the motoring organizations. You should also affix a GB, USA or other national plate as appropriate to the rear of your car. It is advisable, though not obligatory, to obtain from one's insurance company, at a small additional charge, a 'bail bond'. In case of accident, especially an accident involving personal injury to a third party, the bail bond affords the additional guarantee that Spanish courts may require and thus minimizes delay.

Roads Spain has nearly 500,000km/ 310,700mi of main and secondary roads, most of them nowadays extremely good and suitable for fast driving. There is also a rapidly increasing number of motorways (*autopistas*), on most of which one has to pay a toll (*peaje*). Ninety-five percent of all Spain's motor traffic is concentrated in and around the big cities and, in summer time, on the coast roads. Thus it is often possible, on secondary, inland roads, to drive for half an hour or more without seeing another vehicle.

Fuel and oil There is no branded fuel in Spain. The whole industry is controlled by a government monopoly, CAMPSA. Three grades of fuel (*gasolina*) are available: 90 octane (*normal*), 96 octane (*super*) and 98 octane (*extra*). Diesel oil is also widely available. Internationally-known lubricating oil (*aceite*) is available at most garages along the main roads, Spanish oil at all garages.

Rules of the road Keep to the right and overtake on the left. In general, traffic emerging from the right has priority. Unless there is any indication to the contrary, this applies in towns and in the country. When a driver is *not* entitled to exercise this right he is warned at the road junction by the sign CEDA EL PASO (give way) or nowadays more and more by the word STOP.

Road signs Most Spanish road signs are those used internationally. But some that are not: DESPACIO = slow; DESVÍO = diversion; PASO

PROHIBIDO = no right of way; DIRECCIÓN ÚNICA = one way street; OBRAS = road works; PELIGRO = danger.

Ungated level crossings On minor roads there are still some unguarded and ungated level crossings where it is the motorist's own responsibility before he crosses to make sure that a train is not approaching. These level crossings are clearly marked with a sign in the form of a large X or with the silhouette of an engine in a triangle.

Trams Trams in the middle of the street may be overtaken on the right when in motion, but on neither side if they are embarking or disembarking passengers.

Headlights White lights are standard but yellow lights permitted. On motorways it is obligatory to use dipped headlights (*luces de cruce*). Even on well-lit sections it is illegal to use sidelights only. Lighting-up time is at sunset.

Use of horn This is forbidden in most of the large towns.

Speed limits On motorways 120km/75mi per hour, on other roads 100kph/62mph. Lesser speed limits in kph (*round* sign, black figures, white background, red rim) must also be obeyed. *Square* signs with white figures on blue background are merely recommendations.

Alcohol tests are now in force in Spain.

Motorcyclists Riders of motorcycles of more than 125 cc must wear crash helmets.

Seat belts must be fitted to the front seats of motor cars and vans and *it is obligatory to use them on all roads between towns* but not in the towns themselves.

Fines for road offences are imposed on a fixed scale and traffic police are authorized to collect them on the spot. For immediate payment a discount of 20 percent is, with certain exceptions, allowed.

Parking Motor cars may be left in the streets anywhere in Spain without parking lights, provided that they are facing in the correct direction. The parking-prohibited sign is a red and blue disc with a diagonal line through it. A blue and white disc (*zona azul* or 'blue zone') indicates that parking is limited to one and a half hours and a note of time of arrival eg *Llegada 1730 horas* must be left inside the windscreen. In all the big towns parking is extremely difficult except on Sundays and other non-working days. Motorists are strongly advised to leave their cars at a garage or one of the multi-storey car parks and do their shopping or sightseeing on foot or by taxi.

Children No child under 14 may travel in the front seat of a motor car.

INTERNAL TRAVEL

Trains The national railway network is known as RENFE (pronounced Renfay and meaning *Red Nacional de los Ferro-carriles Españoles*). There is a basic first or second class fare according to distance, with supplements for fast trains and for reserving seats in advance. The fast trains are known as *Talgo, Ter* and *Electrotren*, all of which are luxury trains with air conditioning, the first two being diesel-engined and the third electric. Those intending to travel extensively by train should enquire about reduced-price 'mileage tickets' (*carnets kilométricos*) which may be used for all journeys over a period (minimum total distance 3000km/1864mi).

Buses In addition to its train services, RENFE has a widespread network of bus services, details of which can be obtained from railway stations. Many privately-owned bus services also operate.

Planes Most of the provincial capitals and other large cities are connected by scheduled air services of the Spanish national airline IBERIA.

Boats Services for passengers and motor cars from the mainland to the Balearic Islands of Mallorca, Menorca and Ibiza start from Barcelona, Valencia and Alicante. London agents for information or reservations: Meliá Travel Ltd, 12 Dover Street, W1.

ACCOMMODATION

Hotels A list of hotels in any particular district can be obtained from information offices of the Spanish National Tourist Department. (See **Useful addresses**). Accommodation at seaside resorts and tourist centres during the height of the season and at all places during their annual fiestas should be reserved well in advance. At other times advance booking is far less essential.

Spanish hotels and motels use the international classification by stars – five stars for luxury down to one star for the cheapest. There are also hostels and pensions, graded only up to three stars. One star pensions, although naturally lacking in comfort, are extremely cheap, always clean and invariably provide good food. In addition there are state-owned *paradores* (maximum permitted stay normally 48 hours), all comfortable and well-run, usually converted castles or palaces in lovely surroundings off

the beaten track, though some are newly built along main roads. Some hotels and hostels do not provide meals (though they provide a simple breakfast) and they display the word *Residencia*, or just the letter R, in their sign.

The prices that may be charged by each individual hotel, motel, hostel, pension or *parador* are rigidly controlled by the Spanish tourist authorities and must be displayed at the reception desk and behind the door of every bedroom. The approved prices are fixed individually for each hotel and vary among hotels even of the same category.

Most hotels charge more during the 'high season'. This usually means the three months July-Sept. But in some hotels, in the ski resorts for example, the increase applies in winter. In some places it is applied in Holy Week, at Christmas or during the local fiesta. Whatever the price, it includes service. (But see **Tipping**, p. 19). Some hotels (quite legally provided this appears on their official price list) add to the bill the small ITE tax (*Impuesto de Tráfico de Empresas*) which they themselves have to pay.

If a guest intends to stay more than 48 hours and to take all meals in the hotel he is entitled to *pensión completa* or full-board terms, which are cheaper, but he must request these on arrival. If he intends to stay for a shorter period or wishes to take some meals outside the hotel he will be charged on a 'per item' basis (but still based on the officially-approved list) for bedroom, breakfast, lunch or dinner.

Breakfast is charged for only when taken. Furthermore hotels are not allowed to insist that a guest 'eats in'. He can 'eat out' if he wishes without suffering any penalty or surcharge for doing so.

Reductions are usually made for children but as there is no official regulation such reductions are voluntary and negotiable at the time of booking.

With rigidly controlled and clearly displayed prices, instances of overcharging are rare. But as a further means of dissuasion from temptation all hotels, pensions and other establishments offering accommodation must keep a supply of official 'complaints forms' (*hojas de reclamaciones*) on which a client may record (in his own language) the details of any overcharge or other cause of grievance. It is an offence for the hotel not to have these forms and it is an offence to refuse to produce them. The top sheet must be delivered or sent by the hotel within a month at latest to the office of the tourist authority in the provincial capital. The second sheet (green) is for the client, the third (pink) for the hotel. In case of difficulty with an hotel a complaint may be made to the local tourist office or direct to the Dirección-General de Empresas y Actividades Turísticas, María de Molina 50, Madrid-6.

On departure, hotel rooms must be vacated by 12 noon.

ENJOY YOURSELF

Camping Spain has approximately 500 officially approved camping sites. It is prohibited to camp anywhere else. A camping card is not necessary but a passport is. There are four categories of camping site – luxury, first, second and third class – and the minimum facilities each category must provide are laid down by the authorities. Even the lowest category must be fenced in, have unlimited drinking water, electricity, bar, fire protection, sanitary and washing installations, first aid box, refuse collection and a watchman day and night. Many also have restaurants, supermarkets, swimming pools, newspaper shops, hairdressers, children's playgrounds, discotheques and facilities for direct connection of water and electricity to caravans.

The prices each camping site charges for various services are also officially approved and these prices must be displayed in the reception office. As with hotels (see **Hotels**) every camping site must have a supply of complaints forms.

A complete list of camping sites, with a map showing their locations, can be obtained from any office of the Spanish National Tourist Department or direct from: Agrupación Nacional de Campings de España, Duque de Medinaceli 2, Madrid-14.

Cycling Each year in Spain there are no fewer than 5000 races and other cycling events – for amateurs, professionals, juniors, infants and veterans – organized by the many clubs throughout the country. For the address of a club in any particular district or a detailed programme of all events for the forthcoming year, write to the Spanish Federation of Cycling (Federación Española de Ciclismo), Ferraz 16, 5°, Madrid-8, or any Spanish tourist office.

Golf There are approximately 70 courses, some of which are used for international competitions. Nearly all of them are in places of outstanding natural beauty. No fewer than 20 are sited on the Costa del Sol, ten near Madrid, eight on the Costa Blanca, eight in Cataluña, five near Valencia, seven at intervals along the Biscay coast and the rest dotted about the country. All welcome visitors and most have caddies, carts and clubs available.

Many have an instructor, a bar or a restaurant and some of them have baths, practice ranges, putting greens, swimming pool, telephone and children's playground.

Hunting, shooting and fishing

Big game In Spain there are ten species of big game – deer, stag, roebuck, ibex, boar, wolf, lynx, mountain goat, mountain sheep and bear. The lynx and the bear are now completely protected. The bear, once abundant, is now found only in the Pyrenees and in the mountains of Asturias and León. The most plentiful species is the deer, which is found almost always in the mountains, especially those of Toledo, Ciudad Real, Extremadura and the Sierra Morena, in national game preserves as well as on private land. In many places, again mostly in the mountains, is to be found the roebuck, one of the fastest and most beautiful of the Spanish species, and in the Cantabrian range and Pyrenees the ibex, nowadays found practically nowhere else but in Spain. The wild boar is very abundant and dangerous to hunt. As for the mountain sheep, it was introduced from Corsica and Sardinia in 1953 and may now be stalked in various national game preserves including those of Cazorla and Cuenca. See **General information** p. 14.

Shooting Spain's smaller game includes grouse (a much prized but difficult trophy), quail (abundant on the stubble after harvest), the turtle dove (so abundant that 400 birds can sometimes be shot by half a dozen hunters in half a day), pigeons, rabbits (very scarce due to myxomatosis), hares (which have become abundant as rabbits have declined) – and most important of all, partridge, the principal attraction for sportsmen in Spain, drawing 90 percent of the participants, both national and foreign. The most common variety is the Spanish red partridge, which is shot in organized drives that have become internationally famous. In Spain also are great numbers of water-fowl which arrive from most parts of Europe to winter. Shooting is possible around the Ebro delta and near Valencia, among other places. See **General information** p. 14.

Fishing Spain is famous for its fishing facilities, especially for salmon and trout. Salmon is found in very many streams in the northern part of the country (Cantabrian range and Galicia). Trout is even more abundant and is found in the upper reaches of practically every river in Spain. Some varieties reach a metre/39in in length and 5kg/11lb in weight. Lake trout can weigh as much as 12kg/26lb. Fish of the carp family *eg* the sizeable barbel and the bogue, are also plentiful both in rivers and reservoirs and may be fished all the year. More recently introduced is the black bass or American perch. Various members of the mullet family are to be found both in the rivers and around the coasts, along with sturgeon and conger eel. Sea fishing from boats offers the possibility of catching grouper, bream and, by deep-sea trawling, mackerel, cod, tuna, bonito and occasionally in summer, swordfish. See **General information** below.

Underwater fishing is permitted around all Spain's coasts and is particularly fascinating in the Balearic Islands, but the regulations are strict. It is prohibited to use explosives, air bottles or other types of Scuba equipment and harpoons or guns activated by carbon dioxide. Furthermore, to avoid accidents, a buoy must always be used to mark the fisherman's position. It is illegal to take shellfish or molluscs, archaeological objects or objects from sunken vessels, or to gather coral. See below.

General information *Close seasons* are decided each year according to local conditions and thus the dates vary. *Sporting guns* (long weapons but not pistols) either smooth bore or rifled may be taken into Spain on a special permit valid for two months and available from the Spanish embassy or consulate in the applicant's country. Alternatively, guns may be bought in Spain on the understanding that the purchaser will take them out of the country with him when he leaves.

Licences are required for all the sporting activities mentioned. Those for underwater fishing, valid for five years, are issued by the Admiralty (Comandancia de Marina), the rest by ICONA (Instituto Nacional para la Conservación de la Naturaleza), but it is best, in the first instance, to request detailed information on procedure from the Spanish National Tourist Office in the country of your residence. (For addresses see p. 21).

Botany and wild flowers, bird watching, natural history, butterflies All-inclusive Spanish holidays for people interested in any of the above subjects are offered by Cox & Kings Special Interest Holidays Ltd, 46 Marshall Street, London W1V 2PA. The main centre is a village in the Spanish Pyrenees, with accommodation (and study) in two modernized 14th-century houses and meals (with free wine) in a local restaurant. On a recent tour 178 bird species were recorded. There is an expert tour leader for each subject, and a tutor for some. Excursions are arranged to

places of interest in the district. Most of these holidays take place May-August but there is one (Mallorca, botany and wild flowers) in March.

Educational More and more people of all ages (though minimum acceptable age in some cases is 16) are combining a Spanish holiday with a short course at a Spanish university. The most usual educational objective is to learn or to practise the language and students are grouped according to whether their knowledge of Spanish is non-existent, elementary, good or fluent. In the latter case studies may embrace Spanish literature, geography or history. Certificates of proficiency or merely of attendance are given at the end of the course.

The courses are held mainly in summer but a few are held in spring and autumn and there are a few longer courses throughout the whole winter. The short courses last three to four weeks. There are normally three hours of classes in the morning and two in the afternoon, but sometimes mornings only to give more time for sightseeing. Tours are usually organized by the universities to places of interest in the district and can include museums, film shows, nearby fiestas, boat trips, sports, regional dancing, wine *bodegas*.

The fees do not include accommodation but the university authorities help in arranging it, sometimes in the university itself but more often in recommended hostels, pensions or private houses. The student is free to stay at an hotel if he wishes.

Courses for foreigners are regularly held at most of Spain's universities, including such famous ones as those of Madrid, Barcelona, Salamanca, Valladolid, Toledo and Sevilla. Fees vary fairly widely. Enrolment has to be made directly with the university but a programme of the courses available may be obtained from the Spanish Institute, 102 Eaton Square, London SW1.

Cave exploring Spain is so rich in prehistoric caves that many of them have not been completely explored, explored at all or, perhaps, discovered. Some of the biggest caves (see for example **Aracena, Artá, Drach, Nerja** and **Altamira**) are nowadays exploited as tourist attractions. Most of the caves were the habitations of Stone Age man. Simple stone tools dating to Palaeolithic times have been found in large quantities. A very surprising proportion of the caves still contain wall paintings of recognizable figures – bulls, goats, wolves, deer, bison, horses, fishes and in one case an injured lion. There are also hunting, dancing and war scenes. Paints were made from earth of different colours mixed with fat. As many paintings are far from the entrances, lamps were obviously used by the artists.

The caves so far discovered vary enormously in size and form. Some are small and simple. Others are huge. One has an area of about 2 hectares/5 acres. One has 25km/15mi of galleries and six hours are needed to traverse them. Another is 220m/722ft deep. Others have spacious rooms connected by narrow passages. Some are veritable labyrinths. Some have to be entered down vertical shafts with the aid of ropes; others you just walk into. Some contain lakes; in one a river rises. A few have stalactites and stalagmites. In one cave 50 human skeletons were found; in another the bones of a bear with the stone lance-head that killed it still in position.

It is permitted to visit any of the caves, unescorted if the entrance is not boarded or padlocked, or by applying to the *ayuntamiento* (council office) of the nearest village if it is, when a guide will be provided for either a fixed charge or a gratuity. The difficulty for the visitor is to know what caves exist in any particular district. The tourist office in the provincial capital may know or be able to find out. The more serious cave explorer could write in advance (in English if he wishes) to the Dirección-General de Promoción del Turismo, Avenida del Generalísimo 39, Madrid-16.

Health spas Altogether in Spain there are 91 spas (*balnearios*), all officially sanctioned by the government. Each spa publishes a detailed chemical analysis of its waters with an indication of their therapeutic properties. Many, especially those with thermal springs, were discovered and used by the Romans. The spas are well-distributed about the country and the most popular of them comprise several separate hotels of differing categories. Many have swimming pools and there are usually facilities nearby for one or more sport such as fishing, sailing or canoeing, golf, minigolf, roller skating, *pelota*, tennis, shooting. Almost all the spas open only for the summer months and are closed the rest of the year. Further details can be obtained from any Spanish National Tourist Office.

Skiing Spain has many excellent skiing centres which each year become more popular with the Spaniards themselves (including the whole royal family) and with visitors. These centres are located in three main areas:

(1) *The Spanish Pyrenees*, in the provinces of Girona (the two best-known centres: Nuria and La Molina); Lleida (Super-Espot and Baqueira-Beret) and Huesca (El Formigae, Panticosa and Cadanchú).

(2) *The Cordillera Cantábrica*, the huge mountain range inland from and parallel to the Biscay coast. Here the two most-developed skiing centres are those of Pajares (prov. Asturias) and Reinosa (Cantabria).

(3) *Near Madrid*, in the Guadarrama and Gredos mountains, chiefly the three centres of Navacerrada, Valcotos and Valdesquí and, further north, La Pinilla.

(4) *In addition* there is skiing in Galicia (Cabeza de la Manzaneda), in the Sierra de Gúdar (Teruel) and in the Sierra Nevada near Granada.

At some of the centres international skiing and slalom competitions are held. At all there are hotels, ski-lifts, instructors and facilities for hiring and buying equipment.

The season normally lasts from December to April or sometimes May.

Horse riding At most of the tourist resorts there are stables from which horses may be hired by the hour. For inexperienced riders there are group excursions, led by a qualified horseman, along nearby lanes and heathland. This kind of riding cannot be booked in advance and is usually available immediately on the spot.

Quite different are the riding holidays organized by such Spanish firms as Rutas a Caballo SA, Agustina de Aragón 14, 1°, C, Madrid-6. The tours, each with a bilingual hostess and a Land Rover for visiting nearby places of interest, usually last 8-13 days (though there is one special 30-day ride south from Madrid) and are for 8-16 people. They cover Andalucía, the Atlantic coast or Madrid-Segovia, mostly passing through countryside the normal visitor does not see. A basic knowledge of riding is necessary. Overnight accommodation is in *paradores* or other first-class hotels. Midday meal is usually cooked in the open. The hostess-guide knows the district, its history and also claims to be able to divine correctly the exact moment when her charges need a whisky or a glass of wine.

Another firm, Cox & Kings Special Interest Holidays Ltd, 46 Marshall Street, London W1V 2PA, also offer 14-day riding and sightseeing holidays with accommodation in a 17th-century house in the village of Alora (Málaga), with air travel from London.

Walking and climbing Most people who go to Spain laze on the beaches rather than walk in the hills. But for those with just a little energy and a love of nature and tranquillity there is no need to go more than half a dozen miles inland to find deserted country lanes and woodland paths. For those with rather more energy there are mountain walks with gentle or steeper gradients. There are no restrictions other than those relating to litter, fire or damage to crops that are self-imposed by responsible people in their own or anyone else's country.

For those with more energy still and an interest in mountaineering there are no fewer than 750 clubs throughout the whole country, many of them owning mountain huts or refuges. These clubs, membership of which is open to climbers of any nationality, are grouped into a national federation, *Federación Española de Montañismo*. Anyone wishing to be placed in contact with a local club would therefore need to write to the federation at Calle Alberto Aguilera 3, 4° izqda., Madrid-15. Additionally the Spanish federation has contacts with the British Mountaineering Council, with the American Alpine Club and with the Alpine Club of Canada.

All-inclusive walking tours are offered by Ramblers Holidays Ltd, 13 Longcroft House, Fretherne Road, Welwyn Garden City, Herts., in various attractive districts of Spain including the Valle de Arán (Lleida), the Picos de Europa (Cantabria), Guadix (Granada), Almería, Córdoba and Mallorca. The walks are graded according to the preferences or energy of the participant.

Wine tours Blackheath Travel Ltd, 13 Blackheath Village, London SE3 9LD, offer a 7-day all-inclusive 'wine trail' based on Madrid (with sightseeing in city and neighbourhood) and Logroño, capital of the Rioja wine-producing area (with visits to wine *bodegas* there and at Haro).

Youth Hostels Spain has over 50 youth hostels, some for males only, some for females, some for both. A few are open all year round, but most open only in summer and a few only in winter. A complete list with full details may be obtained from: Delegación Nacional de la Juventud, José Ortega y Gasset 71, Madrid-16, or any Spanish tourist office.

EATING AND DRINKING

Restaurants In the same way that hotels are classified with one to five stars, restaurants are classified with one to five forks. Two or three fork restaurants are by all normal standards excellent, one fork without frills but good value, four or five forks outstanding in cuisine, service and

comfort but as a rule less typically Spanish.

It is unlikely that you will get a warmed plate (though there is on record the case of the resident Englishman whose insistence that he *always* wanted a warmed plate was at last rewarded and he got one for his salad too). Nor are you likely to get a side plate for your bread. The bread goes on the tablecloth, which is hygienic enough as the cloths are always changed for each customer.

You will never get salad cream – oil and vinegar are universal. If you wish to demonstrate your knowledge of Spanish etiquette you may place your knife and fork on the table beside your plate ready for the next course, but to show his knowledge of the etiquette of the foreigner the waiter may well pick them up again and replace them.

Meal times Spaniards have always taken their meals considerably later than is usual in other countries but the huge influx of tourists accustomed to eating much earlier has brought changes. Breakfast (*desayuno*), for example, usually of the simple continental type – coffee or tea with roll or *croissant*, butter and jam – is nowadays available in hotels as early as 0800 but may go on until 1100. Lunch (*comida* or *almuerzo*) is now served at 1300 to 1600. Spaniards never take afternoon tea, though it can be found in hotels and cafés patronized by foreigners. The evening meal (*cena*) which it was formerly impossible to have before 2100 or even 2200 can now, at any rate in the tourist areas, be taken at 2030 or even 2000, but it will still go on until midnight, with Spaniards arriving up to then and being greeted uncomplainingly by ever-willing waiters.

Food Contrary to popular misconception, Spanish food is seldom overseasoned with garlic. Nor is it greasy. It is, of course, invariably cooked in olive oil. But oil is far less greasy than butter or lard and far more digestible.

Because many people are prejudiced against dishes they are not accustomed to encountering in their own country, Spanish hotel owners have evolved a sort of 'international' menu which can offend nobody. This has caused the disappearance from hotel menus of the really typical Spanish dishes, which can now be sampled almost solely in restaurants where the Spaniards themselves eat. The best of these restaurants are to be found in back streets and usually have unprepossessing exteriors. Some of the state-owned *paradores* also, however, make a point of serving regional dishes and often print a description on their menus.

Paella and squid   There are a number of Spanish dishes, some national, some regional, which the visitor is recommended to try. The most famous of all the national dishes is *paella*. Its basis is rice and indeed more often than not it is listed on the menu as just rice (*arroz*). Its other ingredients vary from region to region. In Valencia, for example, where it is claimed that the local *paella* is the best in Spain, it contains pieces of pork, chicken fried to a crispness, French beans, peas, saffron. On the Costa Brava and elsewhere they add mussels, prawns, crayfish, squid, octopus, pimiento and claim that *their* paella is far better than in Valencia. *Paella* is served in an iron pan with the ingredients arranged colourfully on top of the rice. It is always cooked to order and takes about 20 minutes. Although it is a substantial dish, to the Spaniard it is usually one course of a four-course meal – preceded by soup or hors d'oeuvres and followed by chicken or steak and a dessert. Also for the Spaniard it is always a midday dish though many restaurants now make it available for foreigners in the evening.

Another national dish is *cocido*, a soupy stew of mutton, beef or pork with sausage, chick peas, potatoes, green vegetables and sometimes saffron, sometimes maize, sometimes pears or quince, sometimes meat balls. The liquid is often served first as a broth.

Omelettes are made in great variety. The traditional Spanish omelette (*tortilla española*) contains potatoes. Other varieties contain onion, ham, asparagus, spinach or mushroom. Squid (*calamares*) are also a national dish. Most commonly they are cut into rings and fried in batter (*calamares a la romana*) but *calamares en su tinta*, squid cooked 'in their own ink', the black fluid which, in their natural surroundings, they eject as a 'smoke screen' when attacked, are a gastronomic delicacy. Then there is *cochinillo asado* or *lechón* (roast suckling pig) especially good in Madrid and Segovia, and *cabrito asado* (roast suckling goat). In many places you will find duck with pears (*pato con peras*) or with orange (*pato con naranja*). *Caracoles* (snails) are universally popular. *Filete de toro* (fillet steak from a fighting bull) appears on menus during the summer. So do *criadillas* which are bulls' testicles, but which a restaurateur in Alicante with a sense of both delicacy and humour translates into English as 'mountain oysters'.

Swordfish and mussels   There is *emperador* and *pez espada* (both sword fish), *lenguado* (sole), *merluza* (hake), *lubina* (sea-bass), *salmonete* (red mullet), *gambas* (large prawns), *mejillones* (mussels).

In addition, trout (*trucha*) from many mountain streams is available in season. There is also *bacalao* (reconstituted dried cod) which, served with a mostly-tomato sauce, is more delicious than it sounds.

Comic opera and cold soup   Regional dishes are varied: in Cataluña *butifarra* (large sausage) and *zarzuela* (a word which means comic opera – it is a comic opera of all kinds of fish stewed together with a gravy of ground almonds, chocolate and spices); in Asturias *fabada*, a substantial dish of dried beans, pork and *morcilla* (black pudding); on the Costa del Sol *boquerones* or *espetones* (fresh anchovies roasted before a fire, traditionally by fishermen on the beach); in Galicia *langosta* (lobster), *caldeirada* (fish stew) and *empanada* (pastry filled with meat or fish with vegetables); in the Balearic Islands *sopas mallorquinas* (Mallorcan soups) and *langosta a la ibicenca* (Ibiza-style lobster); in Madrid *callos* (tripe) cooked with calf's foot, tomato, pimiento and garlic; in Logroño *perdiz* (partridge) cooked in chocolate; in Aragón *cordero a la chilindrón* (lamb braised with tomato, pimiento and onion); in San Sebastián sardines grilled over a brazier in the street and eaten in the fingers. In Andalucía – and more and more in the rest of Spain, where its fame is spreading – you can try during the summer months *gazpacho andaluz*, a delicious ice-cold soup to which *tostones* (croûtons), chopped pimiento and chopped cucumber are added at the time of serving.

Dessert dishes   are not very varied. Fresh fruit, *flan* (caramel cream), tinned peaches and ice-cream (including *tarta helada* or ice-cream cake, usually excellent) are the most common. But around Christmas Spanish *turrón jijona* is delicious and recommended. It is a sweetmeat made from ground almonds, orange blossom honey, sugar and white of egg. There is also *turrón Alicante* (a sort of nougat), *turrón de yema* (made with egg yolks) and *turrón marzapán* (marzipan). Alternatively, try *carne de membrillo* (quince jelly).

And when the meal is over and you want the bill: 'La cuenta, por favor.'

Bars and snack bars,   as distinct from restaurants, can provide a no-frills meal of what the Spaniards call *platos combinados*, which are the sort of ham-salad-and-cheese dishes served in snack bars everywhere. Also there are hamburgers (*hamburguesas*), 'hot dogs' (translated literally as *perros calientes*) and a hot toast sandwich of ham and cheese known for some reason as a *bikini*.

But the most fascinating snacks in Spain are the delicious *tapas*, eaten in bars, especially on Sundays and other fiestas, to keep the appetite happy while it is waiting for the huge midday meal. There are *pinchos morunos* ('Moroccan pins', little pieces of meat on skewers), *chorizo* (a highly seasoned sausage), *aceitunas* (olives), hot, grilled sardines, *anchoas* (anchovies), *alcachofas* (pickled artichokes), *atún* (tunny fish), *caracoles* (snails), *percebes* (barnacles), *mejillones* (mussels), *champiñones* (mushrooms), *jamón crudo* (raw ham), *calamares* (squid), *pulpo* (octopus), *albóndigas* (meat balls), *ensalada rusa* or *ensaladilla* (both Russian salad) and many other things, served in dainty portions and washed down with small glasses of cheap wine.

In the larger towns, bars selling the best *tapas* are to be found grouped together in narrow streets in the old quarter – for example around the Puerta del Sol in Madrid, the Ramblas and Barrio Chino in Barcelona, the Calle de las Sierpes in Sevilla – and it is a ritual to move from one crowded bar to another sampling competitive offerings. Most Anglo-Saxons will find that this fascinating peregrination kills all interest in an intended lunch, but, well, that doesn't matter, for the cult of the midday *tapas* – dropping bones, olive pips, shrimp heads, used paper serviettes and cigar stubs ankle-deep on the floor – is as typically Spanish as mule carts and castanets.

Wine, champagne, cider   *Vino corriente*, the cheap local wine that can be bought in the *bodegas* or wine stores straight from the barrel, is not only cheap but invariably good. The same wine is served in restaurants but the price will naturally be at least treble. In the 'typical' restaurants, if you order *vino corriente* or *vino de la casa* (wine of the house) it will most probably be served either in a jug or in a *porrón*, which is a triangular-shaped glass receptacle with a long spout. Spaniards drink from the *porrón* by directing a fine jet of wine from the spout straight down their throats, sometimes holding the *porrón* at arm's length and even letting the wine hit their forehead and trickle down their cheek into their mouth if they notice they have an audience of intrigued foreign visitors. Just one *porrón* is used by the whole party and as it never touches the lips the process is perfectly hygienic. On journeys, a leather *bota*, which gives a similar jet of wine, is often carried slung over the shoulder and on building sites, farms and other places of work a round-shaped *botijo*, made of porous earthenware to act through evaporation as a primitive refrigerator, is similarly used, though this type of receptacle is for water and not wine.

White wine is *vino blanco*, red wine *vino tinto* and rosé is *vino rosado*. Dry is *seco*, medium dry *medio seco* and sweet *dulce*. There are many Spanish vintage wines which, despite the prognostications of the wine snobs, are just as good as the French. Spain's best wine-growing district is the Rioja, centred on the town of Logroño. Two typical Rioja wines are *Diamante* (white and slightly sweet) and *Marqués de Riscal* (a light red wine with a delicate bouquet). Other famous wine-producing districts are the Mancha (*Valdepeñas* wines), Vilafranca del Penedès (home also of Spanish champagne) and Tarragona, noted for its strong red wine *Priorato*. In Cataluña try *Perelada, Torres* or *Alella* wines; in Asturias *chacolí; in* Galicia the slightly fizzy *Rosal* or the red or white *Ribeiro* served in porcelain cups.

A very pleasant drink to accompany meals in hot weather is *sangría*, made of red wine, water, slices of orange or lemon and chunks of ice and sweetened with sugar or liqueur. Spanish champagne (*champán*) is cheap and good. One of the best brands is *Codorníu* and two good, cheaper ones *Rondel* and *Delapierre*. Cider (*sidra*) is rare and in its elaborately-bottled presentation more expensive than champagne. The two best-known brands are *El Gaitero* and *Mayador*, both excellent and both from the little town of Villaviciosa in Asturias. But in Asturias itself, where nearly all Spanish cider comes from, everybody drinks it in its far cheaper and rougher form. In the *sidrerías* (cider bars) they aerate it for you into a wide-topped glass from a bottle held above the head.

Soft drinks   Water nowadays in Spain, at any rate in the larger towns, is perfectly wholesome. Nevertheless most Spaniards drink bottled spa water (*agua mineral*) which is available in every restaurant either carbonated (*con gas*) or still (*sin gas*). There are innumerable brands of beer, which are good. Other long drinks include Coca Cola, Pepsi Cola, *naranjada* (orangeade), *limonada* (lemonade). Many Spaniards, especially Spanish women, drink red wine diluted with water or soda water (*sifón*). An unusual and typically Spanish non-alcoholic drink sold in cafés and popular with children is *horchata de chufa*, made of ground tiger nuts.

Aperitivos   For sherry, see below. There are many Spanish brands of gin (*ginebra*), among the best being *Larios* and *Rives*. Internationally-known brands are also available but cost more. To go with it there is *Martini* or *Cinzano*, *Schweppes* tonic water (*agua tónica*) or Canada Dry. All the best brands of Scotch whisky are on sale as well as much cheaper Spanish brands such as DYC.

Licores Three good makes of Spanish brandy (*coñac*), all sweeter than the French and far cheaper, are *Terry*, *Osborne* and *Fundador*. Somewhat drier brandies are *Mascaró, Magno, Carlos III* and the outstandingly good *Carlos I* and *Torres Hors d'Age*. Spanish liqueurs: *Cuarenta-y-Tres* ('43'), golden in colour and very sweet, *anis* or *anisete* (aniseed), *peppermint* (crème de menthe), *Calisay* and *ron* (rum). Many French liqueurs (*Cointreau, Chartreuse, Benedictine*) are made in Spain under licence and are cheaper than in France. After a meal try *Málaga* or *moscatel*, both made from the sweet grapes grown in eastern Andalucía, or *carajillo de coñac* (black coffee, brandy and sugar).

Sherry

Sherry is 100 percent Spanish. Spain has as much right to the exclusive title of sherry as France has to that of champagne, and so-called sherries from all other countries are imitations. It is made only in the province of Cádiz, chiefly around the town of Jerez de la Frontera, a name that its original, non-linguistic British importers mispronounced and abbreviated to 'sherry'.

In an area of 50,000 acres there are 100 million vines. Some 130 million litres of sherry are produced each year, eighty percent of which is exported, Britain taking two-thirds. The grapes are still pressed by treading and the *mosto*, or juice, begins to ferment within six hours, very often on the way to the *bodega* from the vineyard. It 'boils' violently for three to seven days, then settles down to a slower fermentation for three to four months.

It is matured by the *solera* system, by which wine drawn off from a barrel for sale is replaced with younger wine. In this way the characteristics of each type of sherry can be controlled and maintained and as it is a mixture of several wines of different ages there is no such thing as a 'vintage' sherry. There are three main types – the dry sherries known as *finos* (*Tio Pepe* is a good example), the *amontillados* or medium sherries such as *Dry Sack* (which is not dry) and the heavier, sweeter sherries suitable for drinking either before or after a meal and known as *olorosos* such as *Solera 1847*.

Food and drink shops The Spanish names for the main food shops are given in the list of key words. **Vegetables** (*verduras*) are bought in the open-air market (*en la plaza*) or, in some towns, there is a covered market (*mercado*). Wine in bottles may be bought at the sign *Vinos y Licores* and wine from the barrel at *Bodega*.

WHAT YOU NEED TO KNOW

Passports Visitors to Spain must have a valid passport. Nationals of USA, Canada, Britain and Eire do not need a visa but nationals of Australia, New Zealand, South Africa and some other British Commonwealth countries do. Visas should be requested from a Spanish consulate in your own country. US citizens may stay six months, citizens of other countries three months but extensions may then be applied for.

Posts All letters and postcards from Spain to the rest of Western Europe go by air, to the USA and other non-European countries by sea unless the air-mail supplement is paid. Although post offices do sell stamps it is usually easier (because of longer opening hours and absence of queues) to buy them at *estancos*. These are tobacconist shops and can be recognized by the brown and yellow *Ci-Tabacs* sign. They are officially-licensed sub-post offices and it is their duty to sell stamps. They should not be confused with stationery shops, which have no such duty.

Letters may be sent to you for collection at any main post office. They should be addressed to *Lista de Correos* (the Spanish equivalent of *Poste Restante*) and should bear your name, the name of the town and *the name of the province*.

Telephones Public telephones are *not* to be found in post offices, for the *Telefónica* is a separate organization. You can make calls either from the telephone exchange (*central de teléfonos*) staffed with invariably helpful assistants or from street kiosks (*cabinas*) which have dialling instructions in several languages.

Taxis (the word is the same in Spanish). In the big cities they are painted a distinctive colour and display the word *Libre* (free) inside their windscreen when available for hire in daytime or a green light on the roof at night. In the smaller towns the taxis do not ply for hire in the streets but there is usually a taxi-rank and even in small villages a taxi-man whose address everyone will know.

Tipping Although service is always included in hotel and restaurant bills it is still customary to tip hotel porters and waiters – as it is taxi drivers, hairdressers and ushers who show you to your seat at cinemas, theatres, football matches and bullfights. Perhaps for waiters a reasonable guide would be eight or a maximum of ten percent of the bill.

Time Except for short periods in spring and autumn when the dates of changing to and from summer time do not coincide, Spanish time is always one hour ahead of British time. In winter it is six hours ahead of US East Coast time (*eg* 1200 hours Spain = 0600 hours New York) and in summer five hours.

Electric current In most parts of Spain 220 volts is now standard but there are still a few places where the voltage is only 125. Even here, most hotels at least have shaving points of 220. A normal British plug, however, will not fit Spanish sockets and it is advisable to buy a small, inexpensive adapter before you leave home. An adapter is also needed to convert North American blade-type plugs to tubular prong. Although Spanish current is 50 cycles, small North American 60-cycle appliances such as shavers and hair driers usually work satisfactorily but electric clocks and other apparatus with timing features do not.

British newspapers are on sale in all the main tourist areas and in the bigger provincial capitals. So also are the *Herald Tribune* and the *Wall St. Journal*. At the height of the season they arrive in the afternoon of the day of publication, but out of season they are more likely to arrive the following day. Their price is approximately three times the price at origin.

Hospital with English-speaking staff on duty 24 hours a day: British-American Hospital, Paseo de Juan XXIII 1, Madrid. But there are doctors who speak English in all the bigger hospitals everywhere. As hospital treatment is expensive adequate insurance is strongly recommended.

Rabies Contact with any wild animals, or dogs or cats roaming free, should be avoided. There is no effective preventive vaccine against rabies. A bite or scratch, however slight, from any wild or stray animal should be washed immediately with soap and water and medical advice sought urgently.

The UK totally prohibits the importation of all animals (including pets) except under licence. One condition of the licence is that all animals are kept in approved quarantine premises for up to six months. No exceptions are made for animals that have been vaccinated against rabies. Penalties for smuggling include imprisonment, unlimited fines and the destruction of the animal.

For details apply to: Ministry of Agriculture (Animal Health Division), Hook Rise South, Tolworth, Surrey, KT6 7NF.

Any animal imported into the US must have a valid certificate of vaccination against rabies.

Churches Spain's official religion is Roman Catholicism. Mass is said in Spanish or a regional language. All other religions are permitted. Services in English: St George's, Juan de la Salle 41, Barcelona; British Embassy Church of St George, Hermosilla 43, Madrid; St George's, British Cemetery, Paseo Reding, Málaga; St Philip and St James, Calvo Sotelo 211, El Terreno, Palma de Mallorca; Church of the Ascension, Sevilla.

Opening hours Bars and cafés are open all day and, where demand justifies, up to 0200. Shops stay open until 2000, 2100 or 2200 hours with a break from 1300 to 1630 or 1700. They normally close on Sundays and other fiestas except at the height of the season in the main tourist areas. Hairdressers open on Sunday and close on Monday. Football matches take place on Sunday afternoons or on weeknights by flood lights. Cinemas and theatres usually open at 1700 or 1730 and again at 2230 or 2300. In any sizeable town there is usually at least one pharmacist's shop (*farmacia*) open all night on a rotation system. **Banks**, see **Currency**. **Restaurants**, see **Food and drink**.

Public conveniences in Spain are few and far between. It is customary to use the toilets in bars, cafés and restaurants and at the more modern filling stations. The Spanish name is *retrete*, *water* (pronounced *vatterre*) or *toilette* (pronounced as in French). Men's toilets are marked *Caballeros* and women's *Señoras*, though often self-evident symbols such as a top hat and a bonnet are used instead. If there is an attendant it is usual to tip him or her (women are just as likely to encounter a male attendant or men a female) with a few pesetas.

Best buys

Among the traditional articles for purchasing in Spain, are shoes, suède or leather jackets, handbags and wallets. Basket-work and hand-embroidered table linen are also good. So are ceramics and pottery. Olive oil is probably the best buy of all, provided that it is pure and not mixed with other vegetable oils. Make sure the label says: *Aceite puro de oliva*. Those who like their oil to be tasteless in salads and odourless in cooking should choose an acidity of 0.4 or 0.5 degrees (*Acidez max. 0.4°* or *Acidez max. 0.5°* on the label). Those who like a little flavour can accept up to 1.0° acidity.

Two other good buys are toothpicks and, for the ladies, a hair-do, which will be cheaper, quicker and stylish.

As for dutiable goods: Canary Island cigars (*Álvaro*) are good and cheap, imported Havana cigars are most probably cheaper than at home and Philippines cigars (*eg La Flor de la Isabela*) just as good and cheaper. An excellent, very inexpensive Spanish made Virginia-type cigarette is UN-X-2. You may also like to take your ration of table wines and liqueurs. Wine from the barrel is not recommended as it doesn't travel.

As Spain is not yet a member of the EEC, the duty-free rations for importing into the UK are somewhat smaller and are as follows (per adult person): 200 cigarettes or 100 cigarillos or 50 cigars. Two litres of still table wine. In addition: one litre of brandy, gin, whisky or liqueur. US customs permit duty-free $300 retail value of purchases, 100 cigars, and, if over 21, one quart of liquor per person.

Useful addresses

Spanish National Tourist Offices outside **Spain** *Chicago*: Water Tower Place, Suite 915, East 845, North Michigan Ave. *Houston*: Suite 4800, The Gallery Bldg., 5085 Westheimer. *London*: 57-58 St. James's St. *New York, NY*: 665 Fifth Ave. *San Agustin, Florida*: Casa del Hidalgo, Hipolita & St George Sts. *San Francisco*: 1 Hallidie Plaza, Suite 801. *Toronto*: 60 Bloor St. West, Suite 201. *Sidney, NSW*: International House, Suite 44, 104 Bathurst St.
British Consulates in Spain *Algeciras*: Avenida de las Fuerzas Armadas 11. *Alicante*: Plaza Calvo Sotelo 1-2. *Barcelona*: Diagonal 477. *Bilbao*: Alameda de Urquijo 2-8. *Eivissa (Ibiza)*: Avenida Isidoro Macabich 45. *Madrid*: Fernando el Santo 16. *Málaga*: Duquesa de Parcent 4. *Palma de Mallorca*: Plaza Mayor 3D. *Santander*: Paseo Pereda 27. *Sevilla*: Plaza Nueva 8. *Tarragona*: Santián 4. *Vigo*: Plaza de Compostela 23.

CONVERSIONS

Shoes

	British	6	7	8	9	10
Men's	European	40	41	42	43	44
	USA	$6\frac{1}{2}$	$7\frac{1}{2}$	$8\frac{1}{2}$	$9\frac{1}{2}$	$10\frac{1}{2}$
	British	4	5	6	7	8
Women's	European	36	37	38	39	40
	USA	$5\frac{1}{2}$	$6\frac{1}{2}$	$7\frac{1}{2}$	$8\frac{1}{2}$	$9\frac{1}{2}$

Dresses

British	10/32	12/34	14/36	16/38	18/40
European	38	40	42	44	46
USA	8	10	12	14	16

Men's Collar Sizes

British/USA	14	$14\frac{1}{2}$	15	$15\frac{1}{2}$	16	$16\frac{1}{2}$	17
European	36	37	38	39	41	42	43

WEIGHT

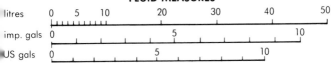

FLUID MEASURES

United States Posts in Spain   *Barcelona*: Vía Layetana 33. *Bilbao*: Avenida del Ejército 11 (Deusto). *Fuengirola (Málaga)*: Edificio El Ancla, Ramón y Cajal s/n. *La Coruña*: Cantón Grande 16-17. *Madrid*: American Embassy, Serrano 75. *Palma de Mallorca*: Avenida Jaime III 26. *Sevilla*: Paseo de las Delicias 7. *Valencia*: Ribera 3.

The language

The Spanish language, known as *castellano*, or Castilian, is completely phonetic, but it has three consonants which do not appear as such in the English language – Ch, Ll and Ñ. It is important to know this when searching for a word in a Spanish dictionary, for Ch will be found between C and D *ie* after all the Cs have finished and before the Ds start and not where one would expect to find it, Ll between L and M and Ñ between N and O.

Key words   This is not a vocabulary list but a supplement to the names and symbols on the maps.

aquarium	acuario
baker's shop	panadería
beach	playa
bridge	puente
bus station	estación de autobus
butcher's shop	carnicería
cake shop	pastelería
camp site	camping
caravan/trailer	caravana
chapel	capilla
chemist's shop	farmacia
dairy	lechería
farm	granja
fish shop	pescadería
ferry (cars)	transbordador
fountain	fuente
garden	jardín
gas	gasolina
gas (bottled)	gas butano
grocer's shop	ultramarinos
	colmado (Cataluña)
house	casa
inn	hostería, fonda
library	biblioteca
market	mercado (covered)
petrol	gasolina
picture gallery	museo de pintura
police station	comisaría de policía
post office	correos
racecourse	hipódromo
railway station	estación de ferrocarril
square	plaza
swimming pool	piscina
tobacconist's	estanco
tourist	oficina
information	de turismo
town hall	ayuntamiento

NATIONAL FIESTAS

The word *fiesta* means a holiday or non-working day. Thus every Sunday is a *fiesta*. It does not necessarily mean a celebration. Nevertheless there are 14 national *fiestas*, or public holidays, most of them the occasion for religious, civic or popular festivity. Shops, offices and banks are closed but bars and restaurants are open and public transport is in operation. Ten of the officially declared national fiestas have fixed dates (though some of the autonomous regions do not observe them, preferring to substitute other fiestas of their own choice) and four have dates which vary.

Fixed date fiestas are: **1 Jan.**, Circumcision. **6 Jan.**, Epiphany or Three Kings. This (and not Christmas) is the day for giving presents, especially to children. It is celebrated in almost every town the evening before, when the three kings (Melchor, Gaspar and Baltasar) arrive in their flowing robes followed by vehicles laden with gifts. **19 March**, St Joseph (*San José*) and Spanish Fathers' Day. **1 May**, Labour Day. **25 July**, St James (*Santiago*), patron saint of Spain. **15 Aug.**, bodily assumption of the Virgin Mary. **12 Oct.**, Spanish national day and anniversary of discovery of New World by Christopher Columbus, 1492. **1 Nov.**, All Saints. **8 Dec.**, Immaculate Conception. **25 Dec.**, Christmas Day.

The four **fiestas of variable date** are: Maundy Thursday, Good Friday, Easter Monday and Corpus Christi.

Holy Week is celebrated in Spain with great solemnity. There are processions (in some places every day) from Palm Sunday onwards. Most famous of all are those of Sevilla where more than 100 *pasos*, or effigies, are borne through the streets and accompanied by barefoot penitents, members of various *cofradías* or brotherhoods in distinctive robes and conical hoods and by Roman legionaries in breast plates and plumed helmets.

The *Corpus Christi* processions also are impressive and colourful and are held all over Spain, the most renowned being that of Toledo. They normally take place in the afternoon and pass over *alfombras* or artistic carpets of flower petals and leaves that have been laid in the streets a short time before.

In addition to the national *fiestas*, almost every town and village has its local *fiesta* and a note about some of them is given in the introduction to each region.

THE BULLFIGHT

Spain has over 350 bullrings. Many of them are in the *pueblos*, or small towns, and are used only once or twice a year on the occasion of a national or local *fiesta*. In the bullrings of the bigger towns there is a bullfight every Sunday during the season. In Madrid (whose ring holds 23,000) and Barcelona (20,000) there is also a bullfight every Thursday at the height of the season.

The season starts in March and ends in October, though in Andalucía it is somewhat longer. Bullfights are always held in the afternoon starting at 1600-1630 when the days are short and 1800-1830 in mid-summer. Tickets are available from the *taquilla*, or box office, of the bullring itself or (for an additional cost of approximately 20 percent) at travel agencies or hotels. Seats in the sun (*sol*) cost less than those in the shade (*sombra*). A good position from which to see a bullfight is a seat in the section known as *tendidos* at least halfway back, near enough for you to get a perfect view. But if you particularly want to be right on the front row ask for a *barrera* seat or second row back, *contrabarrera*.

To avoid the crush it is best to arrive at least half an hour early. As most seats are of bare wood or concrete you can hire a cushion (*almohadilla*) on the way in and don't forget to tip with a few pesetas the attendant who shows you to your seat.

In a normal bullfight three matadors each kill two bulls and the whole bullfight lasts about one and a half hours. Sometimes a seventh bull is killed by a *rejoneador* on horseback. On the posters the bullfight will be described either as a *corrida* or as a *novillada*. There is no difference between the two in procedure, duration or excitement. It is merely that in a *corrida* the bulls (*toros*) are bigger (four to five years) and are killed by fully-fledged matadors (*matadores de toros*) whereas in a *novillada* the bulls (*novillos*) are three to four years old and are killed by more junior matadors (*novilleros* or *matadores de novillos*).

Punctually at the time announced the bullfight will start. It is the only thing in Spain that does start on time (even if, occasionally, in the cause of honour and reputation, they have to stop the bullring clock). The man who controls the proceedings from start to finish is the president. You will find him fairly high up in the centre of the shade. Watch him from time to time, as he signals with his handkerchief for one phase to finish and

the next to start. His first signal will be for the *paseillo*, or preliminary procession, to begin. In the bigger rings the procession will be headed by two *alguacilillos*, or constables, on horseback and in medieval costume. They take no part in the actual bullfight. Behind them in procession will be the three matadors in line abreast, each followed by his three *peones* or *cuadrilla* or assistants. All wear the glittering *trajes de luces*, or 'suits of lights', with a pigtail, the hallmark of the bullfighter, clipped on the back of the head beneath the *montera*, the black hat.

Behind them will be the picadors, on horseback and wearing beaver hats and metal leg guards, behind them again the ring servants, or *monosabios* (literally 'wise monkeys'), and the mule-team. When the matadors and their assistants have bowed to the president they disperse into the *callejón*, or passageway, that encircles the ring behind the wooden barrier. In this passageway are the police, the doctors, representatives of the management, press photographers, the matadors' personal servants (*mozos de estoque*) and sometimes their managers.

The president's handkerchief signal is relayed by the drums and the bugles and into the ring comes the first bull. In a *corrida* it weighs 500kg/half a ton. It has been brought to the plaza a day or two before, cooped up in a metal crate on a lorry. It has been bred and selected for one thing – bravery – and knows no fear now or ever, though it has only 15 minutes left to live.

In a bullfight there are four phases. The **first phase** is short – just long enough for the matador to assess the bull and study its vices as his assistants (or he himself if he wishes) play it gingerly with their capes from the proximity of the *burladeros*, which are short sections of the barrier set forward sufficiently for a man (but not a bull) to squeeze through.

Phase two is the phase of the picadors, the phase that nobody likes – the knowledgeable *aficionados* because, not having to fight the bull themselves, they want its strength preserved, the tourists because the steel-tipped *pic* draws blood and sometimes plenty of it and because the picador's horse receives a buffeting. But they needn't worry unduly about the horse which is protected nowadays with a thick, mattress-like *peto* that the bull's horns cannot penetrate. It will probably be knocked over. It may, occasionally, be tossed right over the barrier and the picador with it, but it is rarely seriously injured. The number of *pics* the bull needs to condition it for the rest of the proceedings is decided by the president.

Phase three, the phase that everyone likes, is the gay, graceful and dangerous-looking (though it isn't) phase of the *banderillas*. The *banderillas*, paper-decorated sticks 70-80cm/27-31in long with barbed steel points, are jabbed into the bull's back in pairs by the matador's assistants (or by the matador himself if he's good at it). Note how the *banderillero*, holding a *banderilla* point downwards in each hand, runs diagonally towards the bull as it charges, making it change direction all the time so that it can't gather speed, and then jabs in the sticks at the moment of near collision. Again the president decides how many *banderillas* the bull shall take.

Phase four, the final phase, is *la suerte de la muerte*, the phase of death. This is what the matador is paid for. In a major ring he'll get £10-12,000 or $15-18,000 for his afternoon's work and unless a goring puts him out of action he can make 60 to 80 appearances in a season. While his assistants keep an eye on the bull the matador formally requests the president's permission to kill. You will recognize him because at this moment he is the only *torero* in the ring not wearing a hat. His hat is in his right hand and with it he makes the *brindis*, or dedication. He can dedicate the killing of the bull to the president, a friend in the stands (to whom he throws his hat) or, pivoting on his heel with his hat held aloft, to the public.

Then his assistants withdraw and he's alone in the ring with the bull. He is now armed with a sword and a *muleta*, a red cloth, much smaller than the yellow and magenta cape he's been using up to now (and which his assistants use all the time), with a wooden batten along one edge. His job now is to kill the bull. First, however, there come the showy passes, with the bull's horns inches away from his body and the crowd yelling *olés* if the matador is feeling good that afternoon, or the horns yards away and the crowd yelling abuse if he's nervous. This should be the highlight of the performance. If it isn't it is not always the matador's fault. If the bull won't charge straight and keep charging there is little he can do. But whether it obliges or not, sooner or later it has to be killed.

The matador's sword must go over the horns and down between the shoulder blades. It should cut the aorta and the bull should fall dead. But if this happens in the bullfight you see it will be a chance in a hundred. More often than not the bull is still as full of fight as ever, even with 76cm/30in of steel buried in its anatomy. The matador can now, if he wishes, use the *descabello*, a sword with a cross-piece two inches from the end, and jab it in behind the ears to sever the spinal cord. Or he can try again with the normal sword (*estoque*). If the process is long-drawn-out he will get more abuse or a warning note on the bugle and probably later a fine. If it is speedy and competent and his *muleta* work has been good too, he'll probably be awarded an ear – or two and even the tail. He'll then make a circuit of the ring to cheers and a shower of flowers, cigars, chocolates, shoes, handbags, hats and leather *botas* filled with wine.

Then the bull's carcase is whisked out across the sand by the mule-team (with cheers or derisive whistles for its performance) and the sand is smoothed and the ring cleared for the entry of the next bull.

GALICIA
(GALIZA)

Galicia lies in the north-west corner of Spain, jutting out into the Atlantic, a geographically obvious port of call on the sea route between West Europe and South America. It has a wet climate and warm winters, so warm in fact that oranges, lemons and palm trees grow. It has a 450km/280mi coastline – on the north to the Bay of Biscay with precipitous inlets, the *Rías Altas*, resembling Norwegian fjords, and on the west from Cape Finisterre ('Lands End' and the most westerly point of Spain) down to the Portuguese border, with gentler inlets or *Rías Bajas*.

Galicia has the most important fishing fleet in Spain, catching cod, sardines and tunny, much of which is dried or canned in local factories. Lobsters, crabs and clams are caught around the coasts and bring renown to local restaurants.

The countryside is green and undulating and dotted with woods of pine, oak and eucalyptus. Its biggest river is the Miño (340km/211mi). Through the centuries the land has been divided and subdivided by fathers for sons to such an extent that holdings have become *minifundios*, too small to be economic. This system and the general remoteness of the region has led to vast emigration to other parts of Spain and to Europe and Spanish America.

Galicia has its own language, *gallego*, akin more to Portuguese than to Castilian Spanish, though Castilian is spoken by everyone. It also has the bagpipe which is traditionally used to accompany the colourful local dance, the *muñeira*.

The first known settlers in this part of Spain, in the 6th century BC, were the Celts, a race, according to Cato, devoted mainly to warfare and witty conversation and, according to Strabo, that lived by stealing each other's sheep. They were mainly tall and fair-haired and in warfare their weapons were swords, pikes, javelins and Boadicea-like chariots with projecting scythes. They lived in *citanias*, houses with circular stone walls and conical thatched roofs. In Galicia the remains of more than 5000 of these have been found. One of them, carefully reconstructed, can be seen at the top of the hill of Santa Tecla, near **La Guardia**, together with a small museum of Celtic and Roman articles found at the site.

For nearly 1200 years the Galician shrine of Spain's patron saint, St James (see **Santiago de Compostela**) has been one of the most important places of pilgrimage in all Christendom, bringing wealth not only to the town but to innumerable places on the pilgrim routes that converge upon it. It is claimed that the apostle went twice to the place which bears his name (Santiago: Sant Iago, St James) – once in his lifetime as a missionary about AD 40 (see also **Zaragoza**) and again after his execution by Herod Agrippa four years later, when two of his disciples rescued his body, carried it to Jaffa, placed it in a boat and sailed across the Mediterranean, between the Pillars of Hercules (Straits of Gibraltar), along the coast of Portugal to the little Galician port of Iria Flavia (today **Padrón**), a journey of 5000km/3107mi that they accomplished in seven days.

At Padrón the disciples applied to Queen Lupa for a plot of land on which to bury the apostle but, being pagan, she refused and handed them over to a Roman official, who jailed them. Released by an angel, they buried the apostle in a stone coffin and when in due course they themselves died they were buried beside him. All three graves remained forgotten for 800 years and were then rediscovered by a local hermit, guided by angels and encouraged by heavenly music. Alfonso II, King of Asturias and Galicia, ordered Bishop Teodomiro to build a church and monastery on the spot and soon the town of Santiago de Compostela (*compositum*, a burial or place of burial) grew up there.

Local fiestas April 28-May 2: Ribadavia (Orense). Festival of Ribeiro wine. Wine tasting. Regional dancing. July (1st Saturday, Sunday and Monday): San Lorenzo de Sabucedo-La Estrada (Pontevedra). Annual rounding up of wild horses and cutting of manes. July 15-31: Santiago de Compostela (La Coruña). Midnight 24th: Mock burning of cathedral front. 25th:

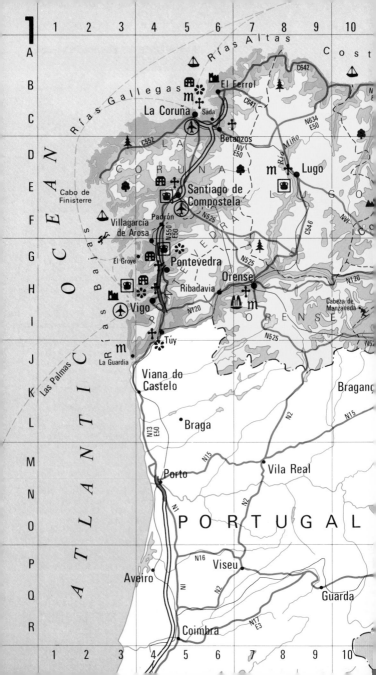

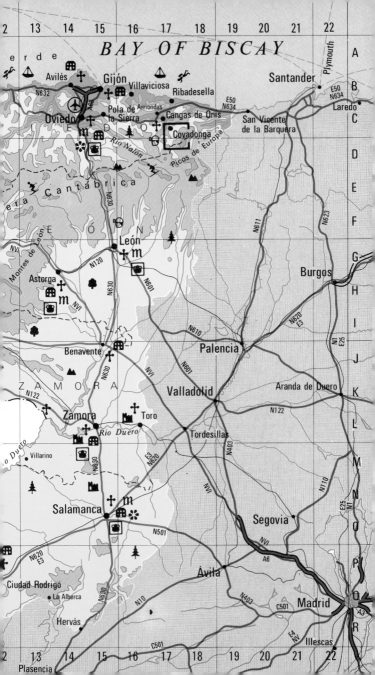

Procession of church and civic authorities to celebrate St James's day. Other days: Cattle fair. Pigeon shooting. Dancing. August 14-25: Betanzos (La Coruña): Fishermen's fiesta. Decorated fishing boats. Battle of flowers. Typical local dances. Fair. August 15-18: Sada (La Coruña). Processions. Fishing boat regatta. Free snack of grilled sardines, maize bread and wine served by fishermen. Oct., 2nd Sunday: El Grove (Pontevedra). Festival of shell fish and crustaceans, both live and prepared for eating. Galician choirs and dancers.

Betanzos   C6

La Coruña (pop. 11,400) The Brigantium Flavium of the Romans, and a port until the river silted up. The Counts of Andrade were lords of the manor in the 16th century and the magnificent tomb of one of them, Fernán Pérez de Andrade, is in the 14th-century **Church of St Francis** (*Iglesia de San Francisco*).

Coruña, La   C5

La Coruña (pop. 232,400) This town, of Celtic origin, is often called the 'city of glass' because of the galleries of windows fronting its houses. It was sacked by Drake in 1589 (the bravery of a local woman, María Pita, is still commemorated during the annual fiesta in August) and defended against the French in 1809 by Sir John Moore, who was killed at the moment of victory and is buried in the garden of San Carlos. ('Not a drum was heard, not a funeral note, as his corse to the rampart we hurried...' as the Irish poet Wolfe describes the scene.)

It was from La Coruña that the Armada set sail in 1588 determined to conquer England. The famous **Tower of Hercules**, though refaced in the 18th century, was built by the Roman emperor Trajan as a lighthouse. In the old town, north of the harbour, are the 12th-century **Church of St James** (*Santiago*) and that of **St Mary of the Country** (*Santa María del Campo*), 12th- to 14th-century.

Ferrol, El   B6

La Coruña (pop. 91,800) Birthplace of General Francisco Franco who until his death in 1975 had been for 39 years Spain's *caudillo*, or leader. The town of Ferrol stands on a magnificent bay guarded by the **castles of San Felipe** and **La Palma** and is one of the country's foremost naval bases and arsenals. *Plaza del Carmen* has a monument to Admiral Churruca, killed at Trafalgar, 1805.

Lugo   H4

Lugo (pop. 74,000) Important in Roman times, Lugo still has one of the best-preserved Roman walls in Spain. It completely surrounds the old town, has a perimeter of 2km/1½mi, 50 *cubos* or towers, an average height of 12m/39ft and a public walk on top. The **Cathedral**, built in 1129, much altered in 1769 though the northern door is from the original building, has 17th-century choir stalls carved by Francisco Moure, interesting cloisters and a chapel dedicated to the town's patron, *la Virgen de los Ojos Grandes*, the Virgin with the Big Eyes. The **Church of San Francisco**, 13th- to 14th-century with very fine cloisters, is thought to have been founded by St Francis of Assisi. Adjoining it is the **Provincial Museum** containing Roman objects and coins. Nearby is the 14th-century **Church of Santo Domingo**.

Orense   H7

Orense (pop. 96,000) On the River Miño and capital of a province that was invaded by the Celts in the 6th century BC and by the Normans in the 10th century AD, Orense has, according to a local saying, 'three things the rest of Spain hasn't – the sacred crucifix, the bridge and the *burgas*, boiling water'. The crucifix (attributed to Nicodemus – see also **Burgos**) is in the **Cathedral**, which has a main doorway copied from the cathedral of Santiago de Compostela, choir railings by Celma, stalls by Diego de Siloé, the *Missal of Monterrey* (1494), first book printed in Galicia, and 12th-century cloisters. The seven-span **bridge** was built in 1230, restored in 1449. The **burgas** are fountains, dating from pre-Roman times, and giving hot water of about 65°C/150°F.

Pontevedra   G4

Pontevedra (pop. 65,000) Among its claims to fame are that it was captured in 1386 by John of Gaunt (who had assumed the title of King of Castile after the death of its ruler, Pedro the Cruel, whose daughter he had married) and that its shipyards probably built Columbus' caravel, the *Santa María*. Today it is a pleasant town of many palaces – see those of **García Flórez** and **Castro Monteagudo**, both 17th-century and housing museums, and **el Pazo de Maceda**, now a *parador* – and many churches – see the 16th-century **Basílica de Santa María la Mayor**, built by the fishermen's guild and having a richly carved west front, and the 13th-century **Santo Domingo**, now in ruins and used as a 'stone' museum (coffins, carved escutcheons, Roman flooring).

Santiago de Compostela   E5

La Coruña (pop. 93,700) This has been a place of pilgrimage since the supposed ashes of the Apostle James the Great were discovered here in 813. A monastery was built on the spot and the town grew around it. Since the time of Pope Calixtus II (1119-24) Santiago has been the world's third holy city, after Rome and Jerusalem, and celebrates a holy year whenever St James's day (25 July) falls on a Sunday.

The famous **Cathedral**, a combination of many architectural styles, has four lovely façades, those of *Platerías* (11th-century), *Obradoiro* (1738), *Azabachería* (18th-century) and *Quintana* (17th-century) in which is the 'holy door' that is opened only at the start of each holy year. When the Moors under Almanzor attacked the town in 997 they respected the tomb of the apostle. But Christian prisoners were made to carry the bells on their shoulders all the way to Córdoba (1000km/621mi) – a process that was reversed 239 years later when Ferdinand the Saint, King of Castile, made Moorish prisoners carry them all the way back again. The ashes of St James are now kept in a silver casket in the crypt immediately below the altar. The *Pórtico de la Gloria*, with its magnificent carvings by Maestro Mateo, is one of the finest examples of 12th-century sculpture in Europe. Juan Dávila carved the choir stalls (1606).

Flanking the spacious main square (*Plaza de España* or *Plaza del Obradoiro*) are the **College of San Jerónimo**, the 12th- to 13th-century **Palace of Archbishop Gelmírez**, the **Town Hall** (*Casas Consistoriales*, 1777) and the 15th- to 17th-century **Hospital Real**, founded by the Catholic Monarchs as accommodation for pilgrims. Among many other outstanding buildings see the **Church of San Félix de Solovio**, oldest in town, built originally in the 6th century, rebuilt in the 13th.

Túy   I4
Pontevedra (pop. 15,000) On the Galician-Portuguese border, Tuy has a 13th-century cathedral that was once a fortress.

Vigo   H4
Pontevedra (pop. 259,000) Spain's foremost fishing port and on the transatlantic liner routes, with the 17th-century **Castle of Castro** overlooking it from a hill, Vigo stubbornly defended itself against the attack of 200 British and Dutch vessels in 1702, was captured by the French in 1808, liberated by the Spanish and British in 1809. The **Cathedral** (*Colegiata*) is 19th-century and the **Pazo de Castrelos** (Palace of the Castrelos Family) in the municipal park is now a museum.

Cathedral, Santiago de Compostela

ASTURIAS

The region of Asturias is a principality, of which the heir to the Spanish throne is prince. It lies in the very north of Spain with 234km/145mi of coastline, the Costa Verde or Green Coast, along the Bay of Biscay and with the mountain range of the Picos de Europa a few miles inland. It has many rivers, all short and quick-flowing, some of them stocked with trout and salmon and many of them driving generators which contribute to Spain's electricity grid. In the National Park of Covadonga, are wild boar, antelope and bear.

Although Asturias, especially around its three main cities of Oviedo, Gijón and Avilés, produces most of Spain's coal and iron, the countryside is as green as that of any British county and for the same reason: rain. It is an unspoilt landscape of steep-sloping pasture and orchards. Whole mountainsides are turned into lawns as men and women with scythes cut the grass and deliver it in mule carts or panniers to the cows which mostly stay at home. You will see also, in almost every farmyard, the fascinating 'houses on stilts' known as *hórreos* if they have four pillars, or *paneras* if they have six, in which grain is stored free from damage by humidity or rats. They are typical of this part of Spain and are so attractive that people from the towns buy them for conversion into week-end or holiday homes.

Local Fiestas   Easter Sunday, Monday, Tuesday: Avilés. Procession of decorated vehicles. Cattle fair. Regatta on river. Tuesday after Easter: Pola de Siero. 'Fiesta of the painted eggs' in which thousands of gaily-coloured eggs are sold. Folk dancing in the main square. July 25: Cangas de Onís. Fiesta of the shepherds. Hill climbing competition. Canoe races on Lake Enol. Swimming. Horse-racing. Lassoing. Regional dances. August (1st Saturday): Arriondas-Ribadesella. 18km/11mi canoe race on river. Pilgrimage-picnic with dancing and singing. Sept. 19: Oviedo. Equestrian events. Opera. Tennis tournament. Regional dancing. Parade representative of Asturias in South America. Sept. 12-16 approx.: Villaviciosa. Apple harvest and cider festival. Canoe races on river. Asturian dances.

Avilés   B14
Asturias (pop. 86,600) This is an important steel-producing town, has two 14th-century churches - **St Thomas** (*Santo Tomás*) and **St Francis** (*San Francisco*) - and several fine houses dating from the 16th century.

Covadonga   C17
Asturias In the midst of the green Asturian mountains, Covadonga has a proud place in Spanish history. It was here that Pelayo with 300 of his followers took refuge in a cave after retreating before the Moors and it was here in 718 that the tables were finally turned and the Moorish conquest halted. In the cave is a chapel containing the tomb of Pelayo and his son-in-law Alfonso I, King of Asturias. Nearby is the 16th-century **Abbey** and the 19th-century **Church of Our Lady of the Battles**.

Gijón   B15
Asturias (pop. 256,000) This busy industrial port on the Bay of Biscay, birthplace of the Spanish author and statesman Gaspar Melchor de Jovellanos (1744-1811), has an excellent beach, several churches, the 16th-century **Palace of the Counts of Revillagigedo** and the **Palace of the Marquis of San Esteban**, 15th-century, rebuilt in the 17th.

Oviedo   C14
Asturias (pop. 190,000) Capital of Asturias, the richest mining area in Spain and the greenest, Oviedo is a modern city of wide avenues with the park of San Francisco at its centre.

The town grew around the **Monastery of San Vicente** founded by Abbot Fromentano in the 8th century. The original cloister is still standing. Later in the same century Fruela I, fourth of the independent kings of Asturias, established his court here.

The **Cathedral**, with its richly-carved 80m/262ft high tower, was started by Bishop Gutiérrez of Toledo in 1388, finished by Arias de Villar in 1490. In it are Pelayo's sword (see **Covadonga**), the tombs of Alfonso the Chaste and other kings of Asturias and the holy chamber (*cámara santa*) lined with 12th-century carved statues of the apostles.

CASTILLA Y LEÓN

In the early 1980s the romantic name of 'Old Castile' ceased to denote a geographical region and became a memory. After 1000 years of history the ancient kingdom amalgamated with the even older kingdom of León – and with Salamanca and Zamora – to form the biggest of peninsular Spain's 15 autonomous regions. But it is one of the least populated, having only 27 people, which probably means five or six houses, to the sq km. It is a region without beaches or any outlet to the sea, for in the amalgamation it lost Santander. It is mostly agricultural, with dry, monotonous, cereal-growing plains dotted with primitive villages of earth streets, clay houses (though not lacking TV) and communal open-air washtubs. In the provinces of León and Zamora many people until recently lived in caves, which you can still see near the villages. Carved out of the hillsides, each cave has several rooms, a chimney and a wooden front door.

There are numerous sheep, descendants perhaps of the huge migratory flocks, each of 10,000 under 50 shepherds with 50 dogs and totalling several million head, that in the 13th to 16th centuries moved through Castile from Extremadura in the spring and turned about in the autumn. The sheep breeders had their own guild, the powerful *mesta*, and you can see today in Soria the houses built by some of its wealthy members.

The climate of the region is extreme, in summer too hot, in winter too cold, but lovely in between. On the southern border are the snowy Guadarrama mountains, the air from which, as it flowed down to his native Madrid, the Nobel prize winning

Town Hall, Salamanca

author Benavente used to say, 'is so subtle that it hardly snuffs a candle but can kill a man'.

In the early days of the Roman occupation of Spain, 200 years BC, the Celtiberian tribes, warlike and numerically strong, better armed even than the Romans, built fortified towns and resisted all attempts to subdue them. No fewer than 54 of these towns have been discovered. The heroic battle and siege of one of them, Numancia (see **Soria**), finds a place in every history book.

Castile is a land of castles, as its name implies. Many of them were built when the area was a no-man's-land subject to incursions by both Muslims and Christians, and conquered territory could not be held until a line of fortifications had been built to protect it. Thus each step in the laborious southern movement meant still more castles.

Local fiestas Holy week: processions at very many places but Valladolid and

Zamora especially renowned. Corpus Christi: streets carpeted with flowers in many towns and villages. June 21-29: Segovia. Dancing in regional costume. Bullfights. June 24-28 approx: Soria. Running bulls through streets. Bullfights. Dancing. Processions. June (2nd half): Hita (Guadalajara). Open-air medieval festival. Bagpipes. June 29-July 8: Burgos. International folklore festival. Exhibitions. Juvenile music competition. Pilgrimage. July 25: Acevedo (León). Colourful pilgrimage. Concerts. Dancing. Agricultural implements fair. August (2nd Sunday but varies): Alar del Rey (Palencia). International canoe race on river. August 15-16: La Alberca (Salamanca). Open-air religious fiesta in colourful local dress. Sept. (Tuesday following 8th): Tordesillas (Valladolid). Bullfight on horseback in open country, with calves played by amateurs. Sept. (Sunday nearest to 21st): Cuéllar (Segovia). 5km/3mi pilgrimage to sanctuary.

Almazán   *map 2*, **K16**

Soria (pop. 5600) Almazán has the remains of 11th- to 14th-century walls with some earlier (Roman) work and three fortified gates; the very lovely 16th-century **Palace of the Hurtado de Mendoza Family** (*Palacio de los Hurtado de Mendoza*) fronting the main square; the **Convent of Mercy** (*Convento de la Merced*), today in ruins, where Tirso de Molina (1571-1648), the friar whose comedy *The Deceiver of Sevilla* gave the world the prototype of 'Don Juan', died; **St Michael's Church** (*Iglesia de San Miguel*), a spacious 12th-century building having a nave with an unusual octagonal roof; the **Church of Our Lady of the Belfry** (*Iglesia de Nuestra Señora del Campanario*) with 13th-century front and a 12th-century image of the Virgin; and **St Vincent's Church** (*Iglesia de San Vicente*), thought to be the oldest in the town.

Aranda de Duero   *map 2*, **J11**

Burgos (pop 27,600) This town has a **church** (*Iglesia de Santa María*) with a fine 15th-century front built by either Gil de Siloé or Simón de Colonia.

Astorga   *map 1*, **G14**

León (pop. 14,000) Famous for its *mantecadas* or sweetcakes (nowadays made also in Japan to the Astorgan recipe). Astorga was a Roman town of some importance and is mentioned by the Egyptian Ptolemy, the Greek Lucian and the Roman Pliny. It still has the remains of Roman and medieval walls. See the **Cathedral**, 15th-century with 17th-century front and porch carved with scenes from the New Testament, and an impressive reredos by Gaspar Becerra; the **Bishop's Palace** (*Palacio Episcopal*) designed by Gaudí; the **Ergástula Romana**, built for incarcerating slaves.

Ávila   *map 2*, **O8**

Ávila (pop. 41,700) The highest provincial capital in Spain (1130m/3707ft) with the mountain range of Gredos as a background, Ávila is still completely surrounded by an 11th-century wall in perfect preservation. The wall, 2½km/1½mi in perimeter, with 88 towers and nine gates, was built 1090-9 by order of King Alfonso VI of Castile to a design by Casandro and under the supervision of the Frenchman Florin de Pituenga. Built into the wall is the apse of the **Cathedral** (started in the 11th century by Alvar García, finished in the 14th) with choir stalls carved by the Dutch craftsman Cornelius, an interesting reredos of 24 panels painted by Berruguete, Santa Cruz and Borgoña and the 15th-century tomb (carved by Vasco de Zarza) of Bishop Alonso de Madrigal Tostado. In the **cathedral museum** is the silver monstrance (1½m/5ft high and weighing 85kg/187lb) made in 1571 by Juan de Arfe.

Ávila was the birthplace of the heroic and very human St Teresa (1515-82), reformer of the Carmelite order and founder of innumerable monasteries and convents. You can see today the first of these (1562), the **Convent of St Joseph** (*San José*); also **St Teresa's Convent** (1636) occupying the site of the house where she was born; **St John's Church** (*Iglesia de San Juan*) containing the font in which she was baptized; the **Convent of Our Lady of Grace** (*Nuestra Señora de Gracia*) where she was educated; and the **Convent of the Incarnation** (*Convento de la Encarnación*) where she lived for 29 years and where a chapel was built (1630) around her cell.

See also the 12th- to 15th-century **St Vincent's Church** (*Basílica de San Vicente*) with its fine doorways (on the south door the carved cornice depicting sin versus virtue) and the tomb of St Vincent who, it is incorrectly said, was martyred in Ávila with his two sisters; and the **Church of St Peter** (*San Pedro*) with its lovely façades, rose window and dome.

Burgos   *map 2*, **G11**

Burgos (pop. 156,500) Birthplace of Rodrigo Díaz de Vivar (c.1040-99) better known as *El Cid*, the colourful, unscrupulous though quixotically-chivalrous mercenary whom time and an epic poem of 3700 verses have transformed into a national hero. He fought against the

Moors and for them. 'They are all the same so long as they pay my price,' he said.

The pride of Burgos today is its 13th-century **Cathedral**, certainly one of the most majestic in the country. It has heavily-ornamented towers, a fine rose window with statues of eight kings above it and the celebrated golden staircase (*escalera dorada*) designed in 1519 by Diego de Siloé. It also has the famous image of Christ retrieved by fishermen as it floated by them in the sea. The image is said to have been modelled by Nicodemus immediately after the Crucifixion and its flesh-like and apparently incorruptible covering (which some authorities say is buffalo-hide) and the spontaneous pealing of the bells when it was brought to the cathedral have endowed it with a reputation for miracles.

Among other treasures of Burgos: the 15th-century **Casa del Cordón** (House of Cord, so named from the sculptured cord flanking its door) where the Catholic Monarchs received Columbus (1497) after his second voyage and where their son-in-law, Philip the Handsome, husband of Joan the Mad, died (1506) of 'fever produced by drinking a glass of cold water'; the 16th-century **Casa de Miranda**, now a museum; the ruins of the **castle** where *El Cid* was married and which the French successfully defended against the Duke of Wellington in 1812; the 12th-century **Monastery of Las Huelgas** (1½km/1mi E.) founded for nuns of noble birth by Alfonso VIII and his English queen Eleanor in 1180, where Pedro the Cruel, King of Castile, was born in 1333, Henry II and John I were crowned in 1366 and 1379 and Francis I of France was held prisoner in 1526; and (3km/2mi E.) the **Carthusian Monastery of Miraflores** (*La Cartuja*), founded in 1441 by John I of Castile and Isabel of Portugal and containing a noteworthy retable by Gil de Siloé gilded with gold brought from the Americas by Columbus. Here the grieving Joan the Mad (see above) kept Philip's body three whole months begging him to awake and respond to her embraces, finally conveying him in an interminable, ghostly procession of torch bearers, praying monks, swordsmen to keep other women away, travelling by night, resting by day, around the icy plains of Castile, her last child (Catharine, destined to be Queen of Portugal) being born along the way.

Ciudad Rodrigo   *map 1*, **P12**
Salamanca (pop. 14,800) Founded and fortified by Count Rodrigo (1170) at the command of Ferdinand II. Parts of Ciudad Rodrigo's walls and ten of the gates still exist. The **Cathedral**, started in the 12th century, finished 14th, restored in 1568, has two fine doorways, lovely cloisters and choir with wood carvings (1498) by Rodrigo Alemán and some excellent wrought ironwork. See also the 15th-century **Palace of the Counts of Montarco** (*Palacio de los Condes de Montarco*) and **Henry II's Castle** (*Castillo de Enrique II*), built 1382 and now used as a *parador*.

Granja, La   *map 2*, **N10**
Segovia A superb palace built in the mid-18th century for the nostalgic, French-born Philip V of Spain after the style of Versailles, containing valuable 14th- to 16th-century tapestries, clocks, porcelain and Brussels lace, and set amid 360 acres of gardens, fountains and parkland.

León   *map 1*, **G15**
León (pop. 131,100) Founded 68 AD as a camp for the Roman 7th legion and completely destroyed 988 by the Moors under Almanzor, León was the birthplace of the Roman centurion Marcellus who, with his wife and 12 children, was decapitated (AD 298) for publicly confessing his Christian faith. It was the birthplace (1256) of Guzmán the Good (see **Tarifa**) and (1535) of the talented gold and silver smith Juan de Arfe whose monstrances are treasured in many Spanish cathedrals and churches.

León has the remains of defensive walls, some Roman, some medieval. The **Cathedral**, one of the loveliest in Spain, is 13th- to 15th-century, but its delicate structure needed strengthening in the 19th century. It has an attractive façade with rose window and two belltowers (70 and 67m/230 and 220ft), a 13th-century cloister, nearly 2000 sq m/21,528 sq ft of superb stained glass and elaborately carved choir stalls. Of the many other churches see the **Basilica of San Isidoro**, 12th-century and with later additions, containing the famous illustrated Bible dating from 960, the tombs of 11 kings and 12 queens and the body of St Isidoro, brought from Sevilla in 1063; the old 16th-century **Monastery of San Marcos** (now a five-star hotel) with its elegant south front, choir stalls carved by Juan de Juni and Guillermo Doncel; and the **Church of San Juan and San Pedro**, modern but incorporating a 16th- to 18th-century façade transported from Eslonza, 20km/12mi away.

Medinaceli   *map 2*, **M16**
Soria (pop. 1000) A small town of much character, where Almanzor, the great Moorish general and patron of the arts, died in 1002. Medinaceli has a unique 3rd-century Roman triple archway.

Medina del Campo   *map 2*, **L7**

Valladolid (pop. 19,200) In the 16th century this was the most important trading centre in the country, where the 'letter of credit' is said to have originated. It still has the imposing 15th-century **Castle** (*Castillo de la Mota*) where Spain's greatest queen, Isabel I, died in 1504 (her body then being carried to Granada, a 21-day journey) and Caesar Borgia, taken prisoner in Italy by the *Gran Capitán*, was held captive 1504-6.

Medina de Rioseco   *map 2*, **I6**

Valladolid (pop. 5100) This is known as the town of the admirals of Castile (see the ruins of the **Palacio de los Almirantes**) and is also a town of churches: **St Francis** (*San Francisco*), 16th-century and containing statues by Andina; **St James** (*Santiago*), 14th-century, with a *Dolorosa* by Juan de Juni; **St Mary** (*Santa María de la Mediavilla*), 15th- to 16th-century with reredos by Esteban Jordán (1590), another by Juan de Juni and a magnificent railing by Francisco Martínez.

Palencia   *map 2*, **H8**

Palencia (pop. 74,100) Here Alfonso VIII of Castile founded Spain's first university in 1208. In 1387, when John of Gaunt, Duke of Lancaster, attacked the town in his campaign to acquire the crown of Castile, womenfolk fought so bravely that the king awarded them the privilege (previously reserved for men) of wearing a band of gold in their headgear. The **Cathedral**, built 1351-1516, contains paintings by El Greco and Zurbarán, some good 16th-century Flemish tapestries and the crypt of San Antolín which is part Visigoth (7th-century). There are several interesting churches, among them

St Peter's (*Iglesia de San Pedro*) with figures of the Rojas family sculptured by Alonso Berruguete.

Paredes de Nava   *map 2*, **H8**

Palencia (pop. 4200) This was the birthplace of Alonso Berruguete, one of the greatest of Spanish sculptors (some of his work can be seen in the **Church of Santa Eulalia**) and of Jorge Manrique (1440-79), the soldier-poet and among the foremost troubadors of his time, whose *Coplars* were beautifully translated by Henry Wadsworth Longfellow.

Salamanca   *map 1*, **O15**

Salamanca (pop. 167,100) Hannibal conquered Salamanca in 220 BC, Columbus visited it to consult the astronomers of its famous university before his historic voyage, Wellington rescued it from the French in a decisive battle in 1812, and today it is a stately city of mellowed golden stone with the loveliest main square in Spain. It is the capital of a province that produces fighting bulls.

The **University** was founded in the 13th century and by the 16th century, when the present building with its elaborate plateresque front was erected under the patronage of Ferdinand and Isabel, had become one of the most famous in the world. Fray Luis de León (1529-91) was professor of theology here and Unamuno (1864-1936) professor of Greek (though Titus Oates, the self-styled 'Salamanca Doctor' was no such thing).

Salamanca has two cathedrals standing side by side and with the River Tormes below. The **Old Cathedral** (*Catedral Antigua*) whose walls are 3m/10ft thick, were started in 1140 and finished early in the 13th century. The high altar was designed

Ávila

in 1445 by Nicolás Florentino and has 53 panels depicting scenes in the life of Jesus and Mary. The **New Cathedral** (*Catedral Nueva*), 1513-1733, has three naves, a magnificent high altar and 19 chapels. In the **Church of San Esteban** (St Stephen), 1524-1610, the high altar is one of the finest works of José de Churriguera. See also in this church the *Martyrdom of St Stephen* by Claudio Coello and the magnificent cloister known as the 'cloister of the kings'. The **Church of Santo Tomás Canturiense** (St Thomas à Becket, Archbishop of Canterbury) was built in 1175, three years after his canonization.

There are many other churches. The oldest, in date order, are: **San Martín** (1103) with a carving of the saint over one of its doors; **San Julián** (1107) containing a retable attributed to Churriguera; **San Cristóbal** (St Christopher, c. 1145); and the round church of **San Marcos** (c. 1178). In the **Iglesia de las Agustinas** (Church of the Augustine Nuns) is Ribera's famous painting *The Immaculate Conception*. See also among many other interesting buildings: the 15th-century **Casa de las Conchas** (House of the Shells) which has sea-shells decorating its façade. The archway through which Hannibal entered the town in 220 BC stood for 2109 years until it was unfeelingly demolished in 1889.

Segovia   *map 2,* **N10**

Segovia (pop. 53,200) At the foot of the Guadarrama mountains, Segovia is almost completely surrounded by a Roman wall with 86 towers and several gates. Its famous **Aqueduct**, constructed of huge granite blocks without mortar and probably the best-preserved Roman monument in the world, 728m/2388ft long, has 44 main or lower arches and 118 smaller arches above, with a maximum total height of 30m/98ft. It is thought to have been built in the time of Emperor Trajan (c.AD 53-117) and brought water to the town until 1908.

Among Segovia's many architectural gems: the **Alcázar**, started by Alfonso the Learned of Castile (1252-84), enlarged by Henry II (1369-79), re-roofed by Philip II (1556-98) using British workmen, restored after fire damage 1862, used successively as fortress, palace and college of artillery; the **Cathedral**, started in 1525, finished in the 18th century, containing retables by Juan de Juni, José de Churriguera, delightful cloisters and wrought ironwork, richly carved choir stalls and 16th- to 17th-century paintings, sculptures and stained glass windows. Among romanesque churches: **San Millán**, 12th-century, situated outside the town walls and undoubtedly the most beautiful; **San**

Martín, la Veracruz, San Lorenzo and **San Juan de los Caballeros** (the oldest and today a museum and ceramics workshop of the Zuloaga family), all 12th-century. Among the many palaces: the 13th-century **Palacio del Marqués de Lozoya** with its fine doorway; the 16th-century **Palacio del Marqués del Arco** with its magnificent patio and vestibule; the 16th- to 18th-century **Palacio Episcopal** with its extensive gardens. See also the 15th- to 16th-century **Casa de los Picos**, so named from the pointed stone on its façade; the 14th-century **Torreón de los Lozoya** (Tower of the Lozoya Family) in the lovely **Plaza de San Martín**; the **Torreón de Arias Dávila**, built in the mid-15th century by Henry IV's paymaster-general; the **Torreón de Hércules**, 12th-century but later restored and taking its name from the Roman sculpture incorporated in it showing Hercules capturing alive the wild boar of Erymanthus; the **Casa de Segovia** (the Old Mint); the 15th-century **Monastery of El Parral**, founded by Henry IV of Castile (1454-74).

Soria   *map 2,* **J16**

Soria (pop. 32,000) Built on the banks of the River Duero and Spain's smallest provincial capital, Soria has much to show the visitor: the 12th-century **Church of Santo Domingo** with an outstandingly beautiful front carved with scenes from the Old and New Testaments; the 16th-century **Cathedral**, built around a 12th-century cloister and containing a very valuable triptych (1559) attributed to Correa de Vivar; the 12th-century **Church of St John of Duero** (*San Juan de Duero*), once part of a monastery belonging to the Knights Templar, now a museum; the **Hermitage of San Saturio** with interior walls decorated by the local 18th-century painter Antonio Zapata; the 16th-century **Palace of the Counts of Gómara** (*Palacio de los Condes de Gómara*) with an imposing front of burnt-sienna stone 97m/318ft long by 19m/62ft high; the **Provincial Museum** (*Museo Provincial*) containing prehistoric and Roman objects found in the province (many from Numancia – see below); and in the park called *Alameda de Cervantes* a large inscribed stone to the memory of a youth who was the only survivor of John I's guard at the Battle of Aljubarrota in 1385 and on returning to Soria was killed by his father because he had obviously not fought as bravely as the others.

7km/4mi from Soria and overlooking the village of Garray from a hill, is the famous Celtiberian and Roman **Numancia** (today excavated and open to view) whose inhabitants for 20 years (152-133 BC) defied Roman attacks and sieges, held out nine months more against 60,000 troops under Scipio Emilianus and finally died of hunger or suicide rather than surrender.

Tordesillas   *map 2*, **K7**

Valladolid (pop. 6700) Here in 1494 the Borgia pope, Alexander VI, apportioned the New World between Spain and Portugal. And here (1508), still in pitiful grief for the death of her husband Philip the Handsome two years before, came Joan the Mad, declining an offer of marriage from England's Henry VII, to spend the remaining 47 years of her life in the **Convent of St Clare** but dying, attended by St Francis Borgia, apparently at last lucid and sane. The convent (in which are still some of her belongings including an organ) was built by Alfonso XI of Castile (1312-50) and converted into a palace by his son Pedro the Cruel for his mistress and future wife María de Padilla while he was still married to his existing wife Blanca de Borbón (who later died mysteriously, suspiciously and conveniently). The Sevillian atmosphere of the convent is said to have been introduced by Pedro for his home-sick María. One of their daughters married the English Duke of Lancaster (John of Gaunt) and another the English Duke of York.

Toro   *map 1*, **L16**

Zamora (pop. 9,800) Toro has the remains of a 10th-century **castle** with eight towers. Among the churches see the **Colegiata** (*Iglesia de Santa María la Mayor*) with three semi-circular apses and a magnificent lantern tower.

Valladolid   *map 2*, **J7**

Valladolid(pop. 330,200) One-time capital of Spain, Valladolid has innumerable historical associations. Alfonso the Learned of Castile married Violante of Aragón here in 1246. In 1469 Ferdinand of Aragón married Isabel of Castile in the **Palace of the Vivero Family** (*Palacio de los Vivero*), which still stands today, and in 1506 his second wife Germaine de Foix, niece of Louis XII of France; Philip II was born here in 1527 in the lovely **House of the Counts of Ribadavia** (today *Palacio de la Diputación*, or County Hall) and from here he set out in 1554 for England to marry Mary Tudor. Born in Valladolid also were Princess Anne (1602), future wife of Louis XIII of France; Philip IV (1605) and José de Zorilla (1817), one of Spain's great writers. Here (1517) the German-speaking Emperor Charles V started his reign of Spain and was presented with a petition (1518) suggesting that it was about time he learned Spanish

and employed Spanish servants in his palace, and from here he abdicated (1556) to retire to the monastery of Yuste, to devote his time to prayer and clock-making. Here Cervantes lived (his house still stands) and in 1506 Columbus, embittered by the non-fulfilment of royal promises, died.

Among the things to see in Valladolid: **St Gregory's College** (*Colegio de San Gregorio*), built 1489-96, with its attractive front and patio and containing Spain's most famous collection of sculpture, including works by Berruguete, Juan de Juni, Gregorio Hernández, Diego de Siloé, Pedro de Mena; the **Cathedral**, designed by Herrera (but built by Churriguera and Ventura Rodríguez, Herrera being too busy on Philip II's Escorial) having an impressive façade, a reredos by Juan de Juni and a monstrance by Juan de Arfe; **St Paul's Church** (*Iglesia de San Pablo*) built to the order of Cardinal Juan de Torquemada (1388-1468) whose nephew was the infamous inquisitor-general; the **Church of Our Lady of Anguish** (*Las Angustias*) containing the unusual image by Juan de Juni of the Virgin of the Knives (*Virgen de los Cuchillos*); the **Royal Palace** (*Palacio Real*) built by Francisco de los Cubos, bought in 1601 by Philip III when he established his court in the town, occupied by Napoleon's brother Joseph when he too, as king of Spain, had his court here in 1813 until Wellington drove him out; and the (11km/7mi on Salamanca road) the 15th-century **Castle of Simancas**, once owned by the Catholic Monarchs and converted in 1590 by Philip III to house the royal archives (eight million items), still the biggest collection in Spain. It was at Simancas in 939 that the Christian forces decimated the 100,000-strong army under the Moor Abderraman III who, on returning to Córdoba, executed 300 of his remaining officers for cowardice.

Zamora   *map 1*, **L15**

Zamora (pop. 59,700) On the River Duero, Zamora was the scene of many battles between Christians and Moors. In one (939) the Moors left 80,000 dead and wounded in and around the castle moat. In another (1072) *El Cid* took part. Zamora has no fewer than six 11th-12th-century churches, foremost among them the **Church of Mary Magdalene** (*Iglesia de la Magdalena*). See the **Cathedral**, part 12th-century, part 15th-16th-century, with its interesting Bishop's Gate (*Puerta del Obispo*), massive bell-tower and museum containing valuable tapestries, including huge one (15th-century) 9m/29ft by 4m/13ft, representing the coronation of

Roman Aqueduct, Segovia

Lucius Tarquinius Priscus (616-578 BC), King of Rome; and the unusual façade (only part remaining of the original 16th-century building) of the **Palace of the Sanabrias Family** (known as the *Caserón de los 'Momos'*).

CANTABRIA

A lovely, green, clean, tranquil, mountainous region with a rainy but equable climate. Jointly with neighbouring Asturias it produces Spain's best milk and butter. Its rugged, unspoilt coast is indented with half a dozen prosperous fishing ports and many sandy bays ideal for the holidaymaker.

Local fiestas June 25-26: Castro Urdiales. Processions. Music. Fireworks. Giants and dwarfs. August (2nd Sunday): Cabezón de la Sal. 'Day of the mountain'. Whistling contest. Tambourines. Mountain songs. August (last Friday): Laredo. Battle of flowers. Decorated vehicles.

Altamira, Caves of   B10
Cantabria Discovered 1868 260m/853ft below ground and now world-famous, the caves contain remarkable Ice Age drawings (15-20,000 years old) of bison, deer, wild horses and wild boar. The caves are closed to protect the drawings but copies can be seen at the local museum.

Castro Urdiales   B13
Cantabria (pop. 12,200) Oldest Spanish town on the Bay of Biscay and one of the most picturesque, Castro Urdiales has the lovely **Church of the Annunciation** (*Iglesia de Nuestra Señora de la Anunciación*) and the remains of the old **Castle of Santa Ana**.

Laredo   A12
Cantabria (pop. 12,300) This is a fishing town and holiday resort on the Bay of Biscay with a spacious sandy beach. From its port in 1496 Joan the Mad (aged 17) sailed for Flanders to marry Philip the

Handsome, son of Emperor Maximilian of Austria (see **Tordesillas**) and from here too in 1501 Catharine of Aragón (aged 15) sailed to England eventually to become Henry VIII's first queen. The interesting 13th-century **Church of the Assumption** (*Iglesia de Nuestra Señora de la Asunción*) has five naves.

Reinosa   D10
Cantabria (pop. 13,200) An industrial town mostly of interest as a centre for exploring the district, *eg* the villages of **Cervatos**, **Retortillo** and **Fontibre** (all 5km/3mi), several water reservoirs and (25km/16mi) the magnificent **Pico de Tres Mares** (Peak of Three Seas) 2175m/7178ft high.

Santander   A11
Cantabria (pop. 180,300) A popular holiday resort with excellent beaches, but with little for the visitor to see. Constant rebuilding, an explosion in the port in

1893 and a disastrous fire fanned by a hurricane in 1941 have largely obliterated the old town. The modern **Cathedral** has a 12th-century crypt. In the **Library of Menéndez y Pelayo** are 45,000 books collected by this famous son of the town (1856-1912). The **Fine Arts Museum** (*Museo de Bellas Artes*) contains paintings by Goya, Zurbarán, Valdés Leal and many others. In the **Museum of Prehistory** (*Museo Provincial de Prehistoria*) are many objects found locally.

It was from here in 1623 that the future Charles I of Britain, then Prince of Wales, set sail for home after discussing with Philip III of Spain (unsuccessfully, for religious reasons) a marriage with his daughter María. Before he left, Santander gave the 'elegant, romantic and disappointed prince' a fabulous banquet (1000 different dishes) which is still referred to.

Santillana del Mar   B10
Cantabria (pop. 3900) This name, the Spaniards say, is a triple untruth – it has no saint (*sant*), it is not flat (*llana*) and it is not on the sea (*del mar*) – but it is a completely unspoilt medieval village (preserved in its entirety as a national monument) and one of the most fascinating places in Spain. It has many fine houses and palaces (one of which, the *Casa de Barreda Bracho* is now the *Parador Gil Blas*) and a superb 12th-century **Church** (*la Colegiata*).

LA RIOJA

'If penicillin cures the sick,' Sir Alexander Fleming once said, 'Rioja wine puts the dying back on their feet.' Here, in this smallest of Spain's autonomous regions, those world-famous wines are produced. There were vineyards in La Rioja as long ago as the 12th century and wine from them was exported to France, and still is, to fortify the weaker French vintages. Here also, in the fertile valley of the Ebro, 90 per cent of Spain's asparagus is grown and, along with pimientos and tomatoes, canned.

Local fiestas   May 10-15: Santo Domingo de la Calzada. Various processions (one including decorated sheep for sacrificing) and decorated ox-carts, one carrying *doncellas* (maidens). June 29: Haro. Pilgrimage, followed by an energetic 'battle of the wine'. Sept. 18-24: Logroño. Wine festival. Processions. Dancing.

Calahorra   G18
La Rioja (pop. 17,700) This town is famous for three things: pepper, Quintilian, the learned Roman writer who was born here c.AD 35 and became tutor to Pliny the Younger; and the great siege of 74 BC in which the townsfolk for long resisted the attacks of Pompey's forces and ate human flesh to keep alive. The town was also the headquarters of the Inquisition courts in Philip II's time. There is a 15th- to 16th-century **Cathedral**.

Logroño   F16
La Rioja (pop. 111,000) On the River Ebro, Logroño produces Rioja wines, the best table wines in Spain. It also manufactures toffee. It was the birthplace (1526) of the artist Juan Fernández (*Navarrete*) and of the brothers Fausto and Juan José

Delhuyar, discoverers (1754) of wolfram, but it is singularly lacking in buildings of interest. The **Church of Santa María de la Redonda**, with its ornate towers, was built in 15th century and restored in the 17th and 18th centuries.

Nájera   F15
La Rioja (pop. 6200) The **Monastery of St Mary** (*Santa María*) was built 1032 by King García of Navarra over a cave where, thanks to the help of a vulture and a partridge, an image of the Virgin was discovered. See the lovely 16th-century cloisters and the church containing the royal pantheons and the entrance to the cave.

San Millán de Cogolla   G14
La Rioja (pop. 500) Here are two monasteries, the *Monasterio de Suso* (on the mountain) and the *Monasterio de Yuso* (in the valley), both honouring the name of St Millán (or St Emilio), a shepherd who died in 574 aged 100, and both containing outstanding architectural and sculptural features.

PAÍS VASCO (EUSKAL HERRÍA)

The Basque Country (which extends across the border into France) is the home of the *boina* or beret and of *jai alai* (*pelota*), the fastest ball game in the world, played by two or four men with a curved, basketwork *chistera* strapped to the wrist to catch and return the ball as it rebounds from the wall of the *frontón* or court.

The Basque people, according to that pungent genius Salvador de Madariaga, are 'stern, loyal, uncompromising and narrow. They are apt to hold fast to their opinions, as people who have not many opinions to spare are wont to do'. They have always been fiercely independent, guarding and fighting for their *fueros* or charters of rights.

The unpronounceable Basque language *euskera*, which to the stranger appears to be all exes, zeds and double vowels, has little literature outside folklore but is nevertheless probably the oldest language in Europe. Unlike Spanish it is not Latin-based. Its origin, in fact, is a mystery. The Basques themselves have claimed it was the language of the Garden of Eden. Some historians believe that it could be the tongue of Spain's earliest known inhabitants, the Iberians, a theory strengthened by the Basques' persistent rejection of the alien tongues and cultures that the rest of the country assimilated from its invaders.

Local fiestas June 29: Lequeitio (Vizcaya). Fiesta of St Peter. Fishermen dance the *kaxarranka*. August 4-9: Vitoria (Álava). Fiesta of the White Virgin. Processions. Bands of music. Giants and dwarfs. Fireworks. Bullfights.

Bilbao   F2

Vizcaya (pop. 433,000) On the River Nervión, this great Basque city of blast furnaces and heavy industry, and with wide avenues and modern shops, was founded in 1300 by Diego López de Haro to whom there is a statue by Benlliure in one of the squares. The **Cathedral**, built in the 14th century, rebuilt after a fire in 1871, has good cloisters and a 16th-century portico. There is an **Archaeological Museum** (*Museo Arqueológico*) in the cloisters of St John's Church (*Iglesia de San Juan*) and, in the park, a **Fine Arts Museum** (*Museo de Bellas Artes*) with works by Goya, El Greco, Zurbarán, Sorolla.

Elorrio   F4

Vizcaya (pop 3000) A fascinating place whose entire old quarter has been declared a national monument., Elorrio has several churches, many attractive escutcheoned palaces and houses, an important group of 9th-century **Christian sepulchres** and nine stations of a unique **Vía crucis** in and around the town.

Fuenterrabía   E7

Guipúzcoa (pop. 11,300) This is a modern holiday resort that has grown around the original walled town whose *Calle Mayor* (Main Street) still retains spacious mansions and whose *Calle Pampinot* has houses of wood. Of interest: the **Castle of Charles V**, attacked many times throughout history by the French, and **St Mary's Church** (*Iglesia de Santa María*), built in the 11th century, restored in the 16th.

Guernica   E3

Vizcaya (pop. 17,900) Guernica has a historic oak tree beneath which for centuries the king or his representative swore to respect Basque rights. Beside the tree is **Parliament House** (*Casa de Juntas*), built in 1826. Guernica's bombing in the Civil War was the subject of Picasso's controversial picture of the same name.

Irún   E7

Guipúzcoa (pop. 53,400) One of the main entry points by both road and rail, Irún stands on the estuary of the Bidasoa, a river that Wellington's troops, reassured by local fishermen that it was just fordable at low tide, waded across up to their armpits on 7 Oct. 1813 to take Napoleon's Marshall Soult by surprise; on whose northern bank French spectators watched the sea bombardment and capture of the town by Franco's forces in Sept. 1939; and on whose no-man's-land **Isle of Pheasants**

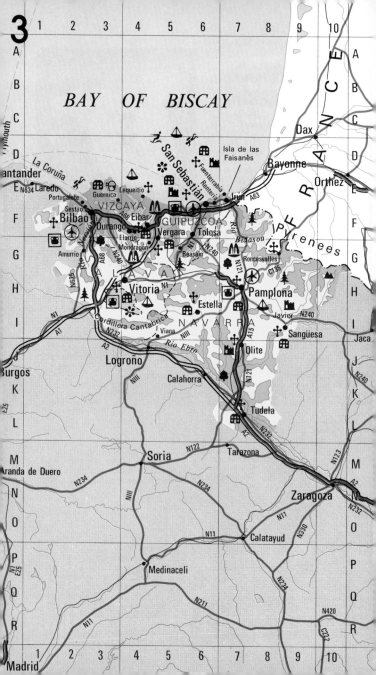

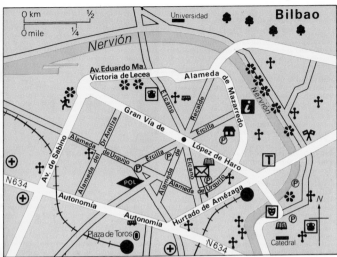

(Isla de las Faisanes) Louis XI of France met Henry IV of Castile in 1469, Spain exchanged the captive French king Francis I for two of his sons as hostages in 1526, two royal brides were handed over (one in each direction) in 1615, and the 'Peace of the Pyrenees' was signed by the two countries in 1659. To Irún's railway station on 23 Oct. 1940 came Franco (one hour late) to meet Hitler (half an hour early and impatient) at Hendaye, just over the border, and to ward off Hitler's demand that German troops be allowed to pass through Spain and take Gibraltar. Hitler – after nine hours' fruitless argument: 'Rather than go through it again I would prefer to have three or four teeth out.' And Churchill: 'Thus by subtlety...Franco succeeded in keeping Spain out of the war, to the inestimable advantage of Britain when she was all alone.'

San Sebastián   B17

Guipúzcoa (pop. 175,600) San Sebastián surrendered without a fight in the Civil War rather than risk devastation of its beautiful avenues. But ironically and sadly its avenues had been built after 90 percent of the town had been deliberately and unnecessarily destroyed by British troops on 31 August 1813 – 'a senseless horror never surpassed in the whole Peninsular campaign', writes Elizabeth Longford in *Wellington, the Years of the Sword*, going on to explain it largely by 'slaughter in the breaches so ghastly that there were not enough officers left alive when the town was entered to control their maddened troops'.

The town nestles below the lovely hills of Igueldo and Urgull and is divided in two by the River Urumea. It has a port, a yacht harbour and one of the prettiest of all Spain's beaches – *la Concha*, the Shell. In the fascinating old quarter are the churches of **San Vicente** and **Santa María** and the 16th-century **Convent of San Telmo**, now a museum containing archaeological and historical sections and paintings by Goya, El Greco, Madrazo, Zuloaga and the 20th-century artist José María Sert. In the newer part of the town is the **Church of the Good Shepherd** (*Iglesia del Buen Pastor*), now the cathedral.

Vitoria   H4

Álava (pop. 192,800) This was the scene of the famous battle (21 June 1813) in which Wellington defeated the French under Joseph Bonaparte (then king of Spain) with the capture of all their arms. Joseph fled over the border and abdicated six months later. In the *Plaza de la Vírgen Blanca* (Square of the White Virgin, patron of the town) is a monument showing Wellington on horseback; and sharing the building known as **El Portalón** with museums of wine and bullfighting is a museum of the battle. Today Vitoria is a go-ahead industrial town producing cars and agricultural machinery, and is famous for its playing cards. It is the seat of the Basque autonomous parliament. The **Old Cathedral** (*Catedral de Santa María*) is 14th- to 15th-century. The **Archaeological and Arms Museum** has Roman sculptures, urns, harnesses, prehistoric axes and 19th-century pistols.

NAVARRA

The beautiful mountain scenery of its northern part, where the Pyrenees separate it from France, gives way by gentle hills and plains of cereals and vineyards to the fertile agricultural zone of the R Ebro in the south. Local industries: canning, printing, paper-making, engineering, shoemaking.

Navarra was for centuries an independent kingdom, except for a period of 278 years from 1234 when its *Cortes* voluntarily chose a French king, Theobald of Champagne. Even when Ferdinand the Catholic forcibly brought the French dynasty to an end in 1512 Navarra still retained an exceptional measure of autonomy. Consequently today there is little enthusiasm for the constant invitation to join the neighbouring autonomous Basque region. **Local fiestas** April 30: Tafalla. Midnight 17km/11mi candlelit pilgrimage of '12 apostles' to hilltop shrine of Ujué. 0400 hours breakfast, return by noon. July 6-14: San Fermín, Pamplona. World-famous early-morning *encierros* or running of bulls through the streets accompanied by youths (often with fatal consequences). The bulls are fought and killed in the ring the same afternoon. Music. Dancing. Cattle fair. Children's competitions. Fireworks. July 24-30: Tudela. Gathering of 'giants' from all over Spain. Dancing. Running of bulls through streets. August (from Friday before 1st Sunday to following Wednesday): Estella. Friday: procession of the famous Estella 'giants' accompanied by dancers. Sunday: Children offer flowers to the Virgin. Procession. Sept. 14-20: Olite. Grape harvest festival.

Typical street, Pamplona

Estella   I6

Navarra (pop. 13,000) A town of Roman origin, Estella was during the Middle Ages the home of the kings of Navarra (see the 12th-century **Palacio de los Reyes de Navarra**) and in the 19th century the headquarters of the Carlist pretenders to the throne. In 1956 the whole district of *San Pedro de la Rua* was declared a national monument. The town has many once-elegant mansions, several palaces and six 12th-century churches. At **Viana** (33km/20mi distant) in St Mary's Church (*Iglesia de Santa María*) is the tomb of the controversial Caesar Borgia (1476-1507), illegitimate son of a pope, who was killed here while fighting for his brother-in-law, the king of Navarra.

Pamplona   H7

Navarra (pop. 183,100) Known throughout the world today for its *encierros* or running of the bulls through the streets, Pamplona was associated 1200 years ago with the historic Battle of **Roncesvalles** (44km/27mi NE) between Charlemagne's retreating troops under the legendary Roland (hero of the French epic poem *Chanson de Roland*) and the enraged inhabitants of Pamplona who had been saved from the besieging Moors only to suffer even more from Charlemagne.

The 11th-century **Cathedral**, rebuilt 1397-1525, with vestiges of the original fabric, has a fine 18th-century front (the work of Ventura Rodríguez), choir stalls carved from English oak by Anchietta, an attractive refectory (now a museum of sacred art) and 14th-century cloisters. Other buildings of interest: the 14th-century **Royal Counting House** (*Cámara de Comptos Reales*); the fortified churches of **St Nicholas** (12th- to 13th-century) in the street named after the famous violinist-composer Sarasate, a native of Pamplona; **San Cernín**, 13th-century; the **Basilica of San Ignacio** built on the site of the castle where St Ignatius of Loyola (1491-1556), later founder of the Jesuits, but then still a soldier, fell wounded in the leg during the defence of the town against the French in 1521;the **Sarasate Museum** containing personal mementoes of the composer; and the **Museum of Historical Souvenirs** (*Museo de Recuerdos Históricos*). Caesar Borgia was Archbishop of Pamplona in 1491 at the age of 16, becoming a cardinal at 17. (Of course, his father was pope – see **Estella** and **Xátiva**.)

Sangüesa   I8
Navarra (pop. 4600) Sangüesa prospered in the Middle Ages by providing spiritual and material comfort to pilgrims on their way to Santiago de Compostela. Among churches: that of **St Mary** (*Santa María la Real*), given to the Knights of St John of Jerusalem in 1132, with its richly carved south doorway and lantern tower. Among noblemen's houses: those of the Prince of Viana and the Duke of Granada. 7km/4mi E.is the **Castle of Javier**, birthplace of Francisco Javier (1506-52),

co-founder with Loyola of the Society of Jesus.

Tudela   L7
Navarra (pop. 24,600) The largest town in Navarra after Pamplona, with chocolate, beet sugar and liquorice industries, Tudela has many fine old houses with carved stone escutcheons. Its **Cathedral** (the bishop's palace alongside) was built 1194-1234 and has an impressive entrance with 116 groups of sculptured figures on the theme of the Last Judgment, a big retable painted 1489-94 by Pedro Díaz de Oviedo, 16th-century carved choir stalls and a 17th-century bell-tower. The 12th-century **Church of St Nicholas** (*Iglesia de San Nicolás*), reconstructed in 1773, has an interesting tiled façade with an original 12th-century romanesque group superimposed showing God the Father holding in his arms God the Son. See **Church of St Mary Magdalene** (*Iglesia de la Magdalena*), built 13th to 15th centuries and **St Clare's Convent** (*Convento de Santa Clara*).

San Sebastian from Mt. Igueldo

ARAGÓN

A completely land-locked region flanked to the east by Cataluña, to the west by Castilla – León, to the north by the highest part of the Pyrenees (over 3000m/9842ft in many places) with France beyond. Descending steeply from the sunny side of the Pyrenees are many mountain streams and several lovely valleys. Those of Ansó, Biescas and Ordesa, for example (see **Ordesa**, **National Park of**) rival Switzerland. The rest of the region, right down to the Universal Mountains where no fewer than four rivers rise – the Tajo (Tagus), the Júcar, the Turia and the Guadalaviar – is flatter, drier, lightly populated and agriculturally poor, growing little but olives and grapes. More fertile, growing sugar beet, fruit and maize, is the valley of the Ebro which runs diagonally through the region. Astride the Ebro stands Aragón's capital and only major city, Zaragoza, industrial and expanding.

The traditional dance of Aragón is the gay and energetic *jota*, usually performed to the accompaniment of guitars or of the smaller *bandurrias*, similar but with 12 strings instead of six.

Local fiestas   June 13: Gallur (Zaragoza). Dancing the *jota*. Running of bulls through streets. Fireworks over River Ebro. July 2-10: Teruel. Giants and dwarfs. Sports. Running of bulls through the streets. Bullfights. Festival of the 'heifer and the angel'. Fireworks. Sept. 12-15: Graus (Huesca). Typical dances, some serious, some comic. Folk singing. Bullfights. Sept. 13-18: Cariñena (Zaragoza). Wine harvest festival. Sept. 14: Albarracín (Teruel). Processions. Bullfights. Clay pigeon shooting. Dancing the *jota*. Oct. 7-15: Zaragoza. Offering of flowers to the Virgin of the Pillar. Processions. Proclamation of queen of the fiestas. Dancing the *jota*. Annual trade fair.

Albarracín   P2
Teruel (pop. 1100) This is an unusually fascinating town standing on a dominating ridge in the mountain of the same name and almost encircled by the River Guadalaviar. Behind the town is an 11th-century fortified wall and a **castle** built originally by the Moor Aben Racín (hence Albarracín) to defend this capital of his own small kingdom. The **Cathedral** on the outskirts of the town, built 13th century on solid rock, was restored 16th century.

Alcañiz   M7
Teruel (pop. 11,600) Its narrow main

street leads up the hill, past the small, picturesque square, the *Plaza de España*, with the lovely galleried façades of the town hall and the old *lonja*, or market, to the **castle** (now a *parador*) at the top. Apart from the lovely little Gothic chapel in its grounds, the castle is 18th century, though a former castle on the same site was built by the Knights of Calatrava about 1179. See the 16th-century **Church of Santa María la Mayor** with its huge porch and spacious interior.

Barbastro   H8
Huesca (pop. 15,200) A market town since Moorish times with an attractive main square and a **Cathedral** (1500-33). It was here that Princess Petronila, aged two, daughter of Ramiro II the Monk, was married to Ramón Berenguer IV in 1137. In the Civil War Barbastro remained loyal to the Republican government, but was captured for the Nationalists in 1937 by General Moscardó, defender of the Alcázar (see **Toledo**).

Calatayud   K2
Zaragoza (pop. 18,000) This was the Roman town of *Bilbilis* where the poet Marcus Valerius Martialis was born c. AD 40 and where he returned nostalgically to die in 102 after spending 35 years in Rome during the time of Nero. During the Peninsular War the town was recaptured from the French by the colourful guerrilla leader *El Empecinado* who after the revolution of 1820-3 was exposed in an iron cage before being executed. There are the remains of an 8th-century **Moorish Castle** and (2km/1mi E.) some of the original Roman walls. 28km/17mi S. is the lovely 12th-century **Monasterio de Piedra** with its tower of homage, partly-original cloisters and reconstructed kitchen and refectory, all set in lovely scenery with many waterfalls.

Daroca   L2

Zaragoza (pop. 2500) The surrounding
13th- to 16th-century wall, 4km/2mi long
(built to enclose emergency pasture as
well as the town) with the remains of 114
towers and bastions, has two imposing
gateways, the *Alta* (High) and the *Baja*
(Low), the latter an outstanding example
of Aragonese military architecture and
bearing the arms of Charles V. Among the
noble houses in the main street is one
where Don Juan of Austria (1547-78) is
said to have lived but never did and among
the several interesting churches is that of
St Mary (*la Colegiata*) built in the 13th
century to house the *sagradas corporales*,
or holy altar cloths (see below), but
several times restored, last in 1962-64. Its
side chapels are partly surfaced with
locally-made tiles, there are 15th-century
alabaster carvings said to be of English
origin ('from the Nottingham school') and
a huge retable dedicated to St Michael.

The legend of the holy altar cloths is
that they were hurriedly used to cover the
host when the Moors suddenly attacked
one day in 1239 during mass. It was later
found that the host had left an imprint in
blood on the cloths and this was consi-
dered to be a miracle. Three towns –
Teruel, Calatayud and Daroca – vied for
possession of them and a donkey was
called in to settle the argument. With the
altar cloths in a box on its back it was let
loose and eventually arrived at Daroca
where, its mission completed, it lay down
and died. In the chapel of the Colegiata
church, occupying the apse of the original
church, is a special chapel on whose altar,
carved with scenes from the miracle, are
the cloths in a reliquary presented by the
Catholic Monarchs. See also, in the
sacristy, the **Parochial Museum** and, in
another part of the town, the churches of
San Miguel, romanesque, drastically restored in 1962-64, though the circular apse
is original, and **Santo Domingo**, also
romanesque but with a *mudéjar* tower.

Huesca   G6

Huesca (pop. 44,400) Here Sertorius (c.
125-72 BC), the dissident Roman general
(who was worshipped by the Spaniards for
his nobility of character), set up a parliament of 300 members to govern the
territory he held in defiance of Rome and
here too he was eventually assassinated at
a banquet by his deputy. The town was
liberated from the Moors in 1096 after
Pedro I of Aragón had killed four Moorish
kings (whose heads were formerly depicted on the Huesca coat-of-arms). See
the **Cathedral**, 13th- to 16th-century, with
alabaster retable by Forment and, in the
museum, 13th- to 16th-century mural and

other paintings; the 13th-century **Church
of St Peter the Elder** (*Templo de San Pedro
el Viejo*) in which is a 2nd-century Roman
sarcophagus containing the ashes of King
Ramiro the Monk, King of Aragón (1134-
37); and the **Palacio Municipal**, built
1577-1612 and containing the famous
picture by Casado del Alisal, the *Huesca
Bell*, showing 12 heads forming its perimeter and one in the middle as a clapper –
recalling the 13 rebellious noblemen
beheaded by King Ramiro the Monk.

Jaca   E6

Huesca (pop. 13,800) Once capital of the
old kingdom of Aragón, Jaca is a walled
town with a massive **Citadel** (*Ciudadela*),
built by Philip II and one of the best-
preserved in Spain. See the **Cathedral**
dating from c.1076; **St Michael's Bridge**
(*Puente de San Miguel*) and the **Town Hall**
in which is kept the *libro de cadena*, a
historic record book chained to a desk.
The unique town hall clock plays a
different and most musical tune before
striking each hour and an especially catchy
one at noon.

30km/19mi SW. of Jaca is the outstandingly beautiful 11th-century **Monastery
of San Juan de la Peña**, partly built into the
base of an immense rock that towers
above it, with two churches and the
11th- to 14th-century pantheon of
monarchs and nobles of Aragón and
Navarra. According to tradition the holy
grail was kept here before being handed to
King Martin the Humane in 1399. (See
Zaragoza and **Valencia**.)

Ordesa, National Park of   E7

Huesca This is an area of great natural
beauty, protected by the government
since 1918, 1000-2500m/3281-8,202ft up in
the Pyrenees, with a dozen impressive
waterfalls (especially so as the snows melt
in spring) and a great gorge that is a
miniature of the Grand Canyon, Colora-
do. There are trees up to 25m/82ft high,
rhododendrons, raspberries and strawberries growing wild and alpine plants
such as edelweiss. Among animals
(though shooting is strictly forbidden)
there are mountain goat, boar, chamois,
fox and squirrel; and among birds eagle,
vulture and falcon. An iron foot and hand
rail erected to cross an abyss by the
English sportsman Mr Buxton in 1881 is
still usable by the valiant.

Saragossa see **Zaragoza** p.50

Tarazona   H1

Zaragoza (pop. 11,200) The prettiest
town in the province, Tarazona is built in a
semi-circle on a great outcrop of rock

Torla, Ordesa National Park

above a little river. A town established by the Romans to exploit the iron mines of nearby Moncayo and occupied by the Moors until they were driven out in 1118 by Alfonso I the Battler (1104-1134), brother of Ramiro the Monk, it became the residence of the kings of Aragón, whose huge palace, supported by brick arches, the bishop now occupies. Above the old town's picturesque streets and rooftops rises the brick tower in *mudéjar* style (built by the Muslims living under Christian rule) of the church of St Mary Magdalene. The **Cathedral**, 13th- to 16th-centuries, has much *mudéjar* work, a 15th-century retable depicting the martyrdom of various saints and an interesting cloister.

Teruel   P4

Teruel (pop. 28,200) The town was destroyed by the Romans (214 BC) in reprisal for Hannibal's siege of Sagunto. It opposed the Inquisition and allowed the Moors to stay and to retain their mosque when Alfonso II of Aragón recaptured the town in 1171, a privilege the Catholic Monarchs withdrew in 1502. The town was occupied by Napoleon's troops in 1808 and was the centre of fierce battles (Dec. 1937-Feb. 1938) during the Civil War when in a single day it withstood 80 air attacks. Nevertheless some old buildings remain: sections of the original walls with towers; the **Cathedral**, built in the 16th century, inexpertly restored in 1685; the 12th-century **Church of the Saviour** (*Iglesia del Salvador*) containing the unusual Christ with Three Hands, **Church of St Francis** (*San Francisco*), 1392-1401, built onto a romanesque hermitage.

But of more popular interest is the **Church of St Peter** (*San Pedro*) where, in 1560, were discovered the mummified bodies of Diego Garcés de Marcilla and Isabel de Segura whose story (much copied by playwrights and librettists) is this: in 1214 Diego wished to marry Isabel but her rich father insisted that Diego must first make his fortune and gave him five years to do it. Towards the end of this time, as nothing had been heard of Diego, Isabel married someone else. Diego returned, now rich, on the day of the wedding, sought to kiss the bride and, being rebuffed, committed suicide. At the funeral in St Peter's Church next day Isabel, full of remorse, bestowed the kiss on the dead Diego that she had refused to give in life. At that moment she too fell dead. They were buried together and you can see their tomb today – *los Amantes de Teruel*, the Lovers of Teruel.

Zaragoza   J4

Zaragoza (pop. 591,000) On the River Ebro, Zaragoza was a Roman town (its name is said to be a corruption of Caesaraugusta) and still has well-preserved **Roman walls**. It was the residence of successive kings of Aragón after James the Warrior had driven out the Moors in the 12th century. During the Peninsular War it defended itself heroically against Napoleon. To the French demand for surrender, the Spanish general Palafox made his famous reply: 'When you have killed me, we'll talk.' But 50,000 of the townspeople (more than half the population) died in action or from hunger. Goya first studied art here (1760-70), having been born at nearby Fuendetodos.

Basílica, Zaragoza

According to tradition the town was converted to Christianity by the Apostle St James the Great himself, as he passed on his return from Santiago de Compostela in AD 40. In Zaragoza the Virgin Mary, then a living woman, appeared to him in the flesh and commanded him to build on the spot a church to her everlasting memory. The church, though rebuilt and enlarged over the centuries, is today the **Basílica of Our Lady of the Pillar** (*Basílica de Nuestra Señora del Pilar*) so named because, it is claimed, Mary alighted on a marble pillar, which her accompanying angels carried with them and part of which, with her image mounted upon it and protected by a silver grille, is still venerated. Many Spanish girls are baptized Pilar in devotion to the legend. The present basilica, built by Francisco Herrera the Younger and Ventura Rodríguez, has two towers, 11 domes and an alabaster reredos by Damián Forment, frescoes by Goya, González Velázquez, Montañés and Francisco and Ramón Bayeu, a painting by Ribera, another by Coello.

The 12th- to 16th-century **Cathedral** (*la Seo*), with its lovely octagonal tower by Enrique de Egas and its *Arco del Deán* (Dean's Arch) forming part of the rear porch, was built on the site of a mosque, part of which remains. It contains a magnificent 15th-century altar-piece, some excellent oak choir stalls and wrought ironwork, the golden cross of the kings of Aragón, 26 15th-century Flemish tapestries and a lectern presented by the Spanish-born anti-pope Pedro de Luna (see **Peñíscola**).

Other things of interest: the lovely **Aljafería**, built as a castle 1049-81 by a Moorish monarch with the imposing name of Abu Chafar Ahmed ben Suleiman Almoctadir Bilah, later the headquarters of the Inquisition, later still the palace of the Christian kings, one of whom, Martin the Humane, it is claimed, here received the holy grail for safekeeping from the hands of the Abbot of San Juan de la Peña monastery, at the instance of anti-Pope Benedict XIII (see **Jaca**, **Valencia** and **Peñíscola**); the 16th-century brick-built **Lonja** or Exchange; the 13th-century **St Paul's Church** (*Iglesia de San Pablo*) with its 16th-century carved organ, main altar by Damián Forment and statue by Mariano Benlliure of the 'Maid of Zaragoza' who fought side by side with her lover against the French in 1808-9 and appears in Lord Byron's *Childe Harold*; the 16th-century **Audiencia** flanked with huge statues and thus known as the *Casa de los Gigantes* (House of the Giants), now the Law Courts but formerly the palace of the Counts of Luna; the **Palacio de Museos** (Palace of Museums) with interesting Roman and Moorish exhibits and paintings by Goya, El Greco, Ribera, Morales and a *Resurrection* (1361) by Jaime Serra; and two mementoes of the town's troubled past – the 18th-century **Carmen Gate** (*Puerta del Carmen*) with bullet holes from the Napoleonic siege and the **Church of St Anthony of the Italians** (*Iglesia de San Antonio de los Italianos*) containing the bodies of Italian soldiers who died fighting for Franco in the Civil War (1936-9).

CATALUÑA (CATALUNYA)

This north-east corner of Spain, separated from France by part of the Pyrenees, has 450km/280mi of Mediterranean coastline, including the Costa Brava and the Costa Dorada. It produces everything from chemicals to cork, motor cars to paper, and 96 percent of all the textiles of Spain. It has also the country's biggest apple and pear farms and 60,000 acres of cobnuts – 'Barcelonas', which come from Tarragona not Barcelona.

The Catalans are thrifty and in business tough. Yet their generosity and hospitality are proverbial. They have a tremendous pride in their history of independence under a long line of counts of Barcelona going back to 874. They celebrate 11 September as their national day – ironically the day they *lost* their independence in 1714. They reachieved autonomy as recently as 1980 and wasted no time in substituting traditional place names and street names for those imposed from Madrid, and especially those imposed by Franco. In your travels you will find this confusing until the world's map makers catch up with the changes.

The Catalans share their patron saint, St George, with England. They have their own language with its own grammar and its own literature. No more than six million people in all the world speak it. Almost all Catalans speak Spanish too but as it is a second language they speak it only when they have to – when talking, for example, to foreigners or to immigrant workers from other parts of Spain.

Unlike some other regions, Cataluña inherited almost nothing architecturally from the Moors, whose stay in this part of the country was short. Instead, Cataluña's main heritage is either Roman (see **Tarragona**) or romanesque, dating from 1000 years later.

The Catalans have an enormous enthusiasm for culture. Barcelona has its own symphony orchestra, the only opera house in Spain, one of the best choral societies, the *Orfeó Català*, in the world, and an intensely nationalistic annual poetry festival in which the first prize is a natural rose, the second prize a rose of gold and the third a rose of silver.

Their regional dance is the serious, unsmiling *sardana*, whose rings were often broken years ago to let a Barcelona tram pass and joined up again when it had gone. The 11-piece musical accompaniment, the *cobla*, is dominated by the *tenora*, an instrument, it has been said, that can laugh and cry with a human voice.

Local fiestas Last Sunday before Lent: Sitges (Barcelona). Vintage car rally. Vilanova i la Geltrú (Barcelona). Procession of couples in regional dress or in masks, led by band. Election of couple of honour. Battle of caramels. Every Sunday in Lent: Esparraguera (Barcelona). Passion play presented by villagers in Catalan language with earphone translations. June, 1st or 2nd Sunday: Calella (Barcelona). Concourse of *sardanas* (Catalan dance). June 23 (eve of San Juan, St John): almost everywhere. Bonfires. July 24-29: Blanes (Girona). Fun fair. International firework displays. Sailing regatta. August 30-Sept 3: Vilafranca del Penedés (Barcelona). Popular festivities. Regional dancing. *Castells* (human tableaux building upwards on shoulders). Sept. 23-24: Tarragona. Dancing of *sardanas*. *Castells* (see above).

Ampurias/Empúries   G10

Girona (pop. 100) An important archaeological site on the Costa Brava. The remains of two settlements – the Greek *Neapolis* of 500 years BC and the adjoining Roman town of 209 BC (the most important in Spain until the rise of Tarragona) – in all covering several acres, were discovered last century and are on view either *in situ* or in the local museum.

Barcelona   K7

Barcelona (pop. 1,755,000) Capital of Cataluña, with 2000 years of history, Barcelona has a prosperous port, much industry, a university, the biggest opera house in Europe after the Scala, Milan, two bull-rings, two huge football stadiums and some of the finest shops in Spain. In the centre is the main square (*Plaza de Cataluña*). Running off it to the north is the wide and lovely *Paseo de Gracia*,

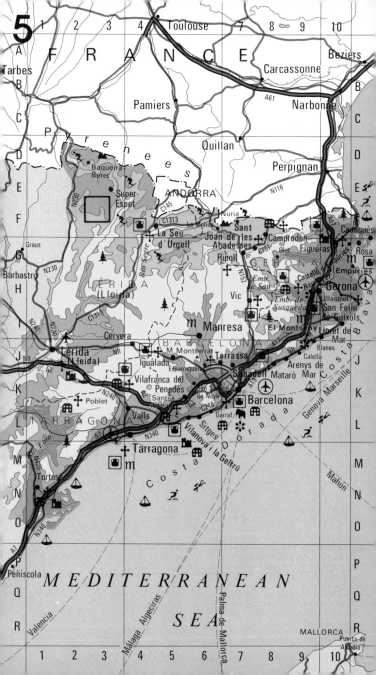

Barcelona's most exclusive shopping street, crossed at right angles first by the *Gran Via de les Corts Catalanes* (or just the *Gran Via*) and later by the *Diagonal*, two of the city's main arteries. To the south of the *Plaza de Catalunya* are the world-famous **Ramblas** forming one continuous *paseo*, or promenade, shaded by trees and with traffic and shops on each side. The **Ramblas** have been described by the Spanish poet García Lorca as the gayest street in the world and by the British writer John Langdon-Davies as a pulse which warns when anything from a football match to a revolution is imminent. On the right is the *Barrio Chino* (Chinese Quarter, though there are no longer any Chinese), centre of the city's cosmopolitan night-life, on the left the *Barrio Gótico* (Gothic Quarter). At the far end are the docks, with a statue of Christopher Columbus (*Cristóbal Colón*) and an exact replica (open to public) of the little caravel, the *Santa María*, in which he discovered the New World.

If time is limited see: the **Cathedral**. It dates from the 13th to 14th centuries, though the main front was rebuilt last century and the dome early this century. The main altar (consecrated 1337) is supported by two pillars believed to have belonged to an earlier church and that may possibly date back to 1058. In the epistle nave is the crucifix believed to have been carried by Don Juan of Austria in the victorious battle against the Turks at Lepanto in 1571. The lovely cloisters lead to the **Cathedral Museum** containing the solid silver throne of King Martin the Humane (1395-1410), the famous *Pietà* painted by Bartolomé Bermejo of Córdoba and donated by Archdeacon Desplá (whose lovely 16th-century house **La Casa del Arcediano** is nearby in Calle Santa Llúcia); several good paintings, sculptures and tapestries and the illuminated missal of Santa Eulalia the martyr (whose tomb is in the crypt beneath the altar). On the choir stalls are the coats of arms of members of the Order of the Golden Fleece who met here in 1519 (including that of Henry VIII of England whose current wife was Catharine of Aragón).

The **Church of the Holy Family** (*Templo de la Sagrada Familia*) of most unusual architecture, started 1882 and still unfinished, designed by Antonio Gaudí who himself supervised the work until he was killed by a Barcelona tram in 1926. The church will have a massive central tower, three elaborately ornamented façades dedicated to the Nativity, the Glory and the Passion, each with four slender, tapering belfry towers.

Spanish Village (*Pueblo Español*), built

1929 for the international exhibition, is a faithful representation of characteristic architecture from all parts of Spain. The buildings are occupied by arts and crafts shops and by artisans working in public view. There is also an **Arts and Crafts Museum** (*Museo de Industrias y Artes Populares*). Not far away in the Park of Montjuic is the **Museum of Catalan Art** (*Museo de Arte de Catalunya*) containing the world's finest collection of romanesque and Catalan Gothic art and murals, 14th-century paintings by the brothers Jaume, Joan and Pere Serra, by the Catalan artists Bernat Martorell, Lluis Dalmau, Lluis Borrassá, Jaime Huguet and by the Spanish artists El Greco, Ribera, Morales, Zurbarán and Velázquez.

Visitors with more time should also see: the **Archaeological Museum** (*Museo Arqueológico*) with prehistoric relics and Roman mosaics; the **Ethnological Museum** (*Museo Etnológico*) containing relics of Latin-American, African and Asiatic civilizations; and the **Military Museum** (*Museo Militar*). All three are in the Montjuic district, as also is the **Fundación Miró**, a museum dedicated to the Catalan artist Joan Miró.

In the Park of Ciudadela are the **Museum of Modern Art** (*Museo de Arte Moderno*) with paintings and sculptures from 1800 by the Catalan artists Mariano Fortuny, Santiago Rusiñol, Joaquín Mir, Joaquín Sorolla, the French-born English artist Alfred Sisley and the Basque Zuloaga; the **Natural History Museum** (*Museo de Historia Natural*) and the **Zoo**; the **Martorell Museum** specializing in geology, rocks and fossils; and the **Numismatic Museum** (*Gabinete Numismático*) with nine rooms displaying coins. Not far away is the important 14th-century **Church of Santa María del Mar** (St Mary of the Sea) and the **Picasso Museum** (address; Calle Moncada 15) containing a large collection of Picasso's works, much augmented after his death.

In the Ramblas are the **Museum of Decorative Arts** (*Museo de Artes Decorativas*) and the **Postal and Philatelic Museum** (*Museo Postal y Filatélico*), both housed in the lovely Palace of the Virreina. The **Maritime Museum** (*Museo Marítimo*) is in the *Atarazanas*, the old ship yards.

In the higher part of the city are the **Pedralbes Palace Museum** containing a good collection of tapestries and the **Museum of the Monastery of Pedralbes** (open Sundays only 1200-1400) containing the famous 14th-century murals of Ferrer Bassa. Still higher above the city is **Tibidabo**, affording a truly magnificent view over the city and out to sea.

Blanes   J9
Girona (pop. 20,200) At the southern end
of the Costa Brava with the hill of San
Juan rising above it and where Jaime
Ferrer, Columbus's map-maker, once
lived, Blanes has 5km/3mi of sandy
beaches, a large fishing fleet whose catch
is dutch-auctioned every afternoon on the
quay, a busy port, an **aquarium** and the
famous **Botanical Gardens** 'Marimurtra',
founded by the German botanist Carlos
Faust and, since his death in 1952, admi-
nistered by an international trust.

Camprodón   F8
Girona (pop. 2400) Birthplace of the
composer Albéniz, Camprodón is a pretty
little town in the foothills of the Spanish
Pyrenees. It has a 15th-century **bridge** and
gatehouse with two streams meeting beneath it and the 12th-century **Monastery of
San Pedro**.

Castelló d'Empúries   G10
Girona (pop. 2700) **St Mary's Church**
(*Iglesia de Santa María*) has an elaborate
12th-century doorway, an altar-piece
(1485) by Vicente Borrás and stands on
the site occupied first by a 6th-century
Visigoth church (destroyed by the Moors)
and later by one built in 888 by Wilfred the
Hairy, Count of Barcelona.

Empúries see Ampurias p. 51
Figueras/Figueres   G10
Girona (pop. 30,600) A pleasant town
notable only (apart from its triple-walled
Castle of San Fernando) for having been
the birthplace of Narciso Monturiol, builder of one of the earliest submarines
(1859), and of the artist Salvador Dalí, an
interesting collection of whose works is in
the **museum** bearing his name.

Girona/Gerona   H10
Girona (pop. 87,600) This sedate capital
of the province whose coast is the Costa
Brava has three rivers running through it.
The main one, the Oñar, with the lovely
Ramblas or promenade parallel to it,
separates the modern, industrial area
(*Barrio del Mercadel*) from the fascinating
old town (*Barrio de la Catedral*).
   The **Cathedral**, consecrated in 1038,
enlarged in 1338, completed in 1456, has a
14th-century main entrance flanked by the
remains of stone carvings of the 12
apostles, the largest Gothic nave in the
world, magnificent stained-glass windows,
28 side chapels, an altar-piece dating from
1325, and, behind it, a valuable marble
chair from the original 11th-century
cathedral whose tower (called Charlemagne's Tower though built 400 years

after Charlemagne's time) can be seen
from the gardens of the 12th-century
cloisters. Many valuable treasures, tapestries and manuscripts are kept in the
chapter houses (*salas capitulares*). The
Church of St Felix (*Iglesia de San Félix*),
13th- to 14th-centuries with 17th-century
main façade, has the loveliest spire in
Cataluña (despite losing the top half by
lightning in 1581), eight 2nd- to 4th-
century Roman sarcophagi and a monument to General Álvarez de Castro, hero
of the six-month siege of the town by
Napoleon's troops in 1809. See also in
Girona: the 12th-century **Arab Baths**
(*Baños Árabes*); the **Church of San Pedro
de Galligans**, an outstanding example of
10th- to 12th-century architecture now
used as the **Archaeological Museum** in
which are paintings by many old masters
(including Luini, pupil of Leonardo da
Vinci) and by the Catalan artists Rusiñol,
Martí Alsina, Armet and Borrell; and the
Diocesan Museum containing some of the
finest mural paintings in Cataluña.

Lleida/Lérida   J1
Lleida (pop. 110,000) Hixem III, the
Moorish calif of Córdoba, died here in
1031 and Granados, the Spanish composer, was born here in 1867. Lleida is capital
of a province noted for its fruit and olive
oil. It has two cathedrals. The **Old
Cathedral** (*la Seo*), built 1203-78 and for
200 years until 1950 an army barracks,
stands within the walls of the old castle. It
has an interesting doorway (*la puerta de
los apóstoles*, the gate of the apostles)
leading to the cloisters. The **New Cathedral** (*Catedral Nueva*), 1671-1781, claims to
possess a 'holy cloth', part of the swad-
dling clothes of the baby Jesus. The **Town
Hall**, a superb building, called *la Pahería*,
in the main pedestrians-only shopping
street, has a 13th-century front and **St
Laurence's Church** (*Iglesia de San Lorenzo*), 14th-century, is built on the site of a
mosque. See also the **Old Hospital of
Santa María**, 15th- to 16th-century.

Lloret de Mar   I10
Girona (pop. 10,500) The Costa Brava's
major holiday resort and the only one
open all the year round.

Montserrat, Monastery of   J6
Barcelona A high proportion of Catalan
daughters are baptized Montserrat, a
surprising name, meaning 'serrated
mountain', for a lovely señorita, but
demonstrating devotion for the monastery
and its *Moreneta* or Black Virgin, said to
have been carved by St Luke, brought to
Spain by St Peter, lost during the brief
Moorish occupation of Cataluña, refound

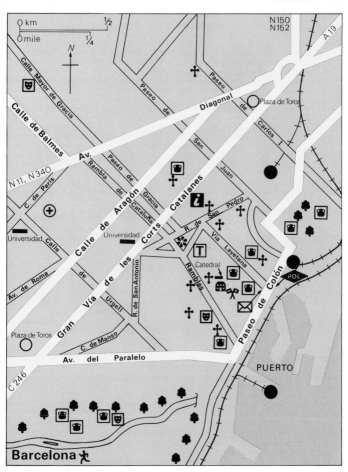

in 880 in the 'holy cave' (open to public) and after many vicissitudes in the Napoleonic, Carlist and Civil Wars installed on her present throne. Another legend is of the monastery's connection with the holy grail and thus with Wagner's opera *Parsifal*. Founded in the 9th century, the monastery is 700m/2296ft up the serrated mountain with a funicular continuing to the top (1300m/4265ft) from which there is a wonderful view.

Olot   G8
Girona (pop. 24,900) Olot was completely destroyed by earthquake in 1427. In the

vicinity are numerous extinct volcanoes, the biggest, called *Santa Margarita*, having a diameter of 2000m/6562ft.

Poblet, Monastery of   K3
Tarragona This shrine beloved of the Catalans was founded for Cistercian monks in 1149 by Ramón Berenguer IV, Count of Barcelona, and became the burial place of subsequent counts of Barcelona who, as a result of Berenguer's own marriage, were also kings of Aragón. But in the peasant rising of 1835 practically everything except the fabric of the monastery was wrecked, including most

of the royal tombs and others containing the complete skeletons of no fewer than 66 saints. Some of the tombs have now been reconstructed by the Barcelona sculptor Federico Marés. The **main church**, started in the reign of Berenguer's son Alfonso II (1162-96), has a truly magnificent main doorway, an altar decorated with tiles donated by Pope León XIII from the Vatican workshops and a huge, mid-16th-century alabaster retable by Damián Forment. The **cloister**, one of the finest and best-preserved in Cataluña, took a century (1200-97) to build. See also the small but lovely **St George's Chapel** (*Capilla de San Jorge*), the 15th-century **Puerta Dorada** (Gilded Gate) so called because its walls were covered with copper for Philip II's visit in 1564, and the 14th-century **Palace of King Martin the Humane** (*Palacio del Rey Martín el Humano*), built over the *lagares* where wine was pressed.

Ripoll   G7

Girona (pop. 12,100) Damaged by earthquake in 1427, today a textile centre, Ripoll has a **Monastery** (*Monasterio de Santa María*) founded in 888 by Wilfred the Hairy, Count of Barcelona, sacked and burned during the peasants' revolt of 1835. The monastery church has a superb doorway surrounded by carving, an altar decorated with tiles made in the Vatican workshops, donated by Pope León XIII, and some of the best cloisters (12th- to 14th-century) in Cataluña.

Sant Feliu de Guíxols   I10

Girona (pop. 15,500) Second largest resort on the Costa Brava, it has a 14th-century church with an interesting arcaded gallery known as *puerta ferrada*, originally part of the 11th-century monastery of San Benito, reputedly founded by Charlemagne in the 8th century.

Sant Joan de les Abadesses   G7

Girona (pop. 4300) An enchanting little town on the River Ter in the foothills of the Pyrenees, it grew around the abbey founded by Wilfred the Hairy, Count of Barcelona (874-98) and his wife Vinidilda. Their daughter Emma was the first abbess. The town was badly damaged twice (1151 and 1427) by earthquake, lost half its population in the plague of 1348, was sacked by Philip V's troops in 1711 and by Napoleon's in 1809. In the **Church of St John** (*San Juan*), built in 1150, choir added in the 16th century, is the famous *Descent from the Cross*, comprising six life-size figures (a seventh figure was destroyed in the Civil War 1936-9) carved in 1290 by an unknown artist. See also the small but lovely 15th-century cloisters.

Santes Creus, Monastery of   K5

Tarragona Now restored after one and a half centuries of vandalism more destructive than 600 years of weather, this is one of Cataluña's architectural and historical treasures. (See also **Poblet**.) The **church**, with its 13th-century façade, contains the massive tomb with ornamental marble cover of Pedro III the Great (1276-85) in the exact position he himself chose, and the tombs of his son James II (1291-1327) and daughter-in-law Blanca of Anjou. In the walls of the great cloisters, built 1313-41, are the sepulchres of Catalan nobles and in the floor of the chapter house those of seven of the monastery's abbots. Above is the dormitory with a ceiling of 11 arches. The so-called **Palacio Royal**, with its two beautiful patios, was the living quarters of visiting monarchs.

Seu d'Urgell, La   F4

Lleida (pop. 10,700) The town has an 11th-century cathedral whose bishop is joint ruler with the President of France of the neighbouring principality of Andorra.

Sitges   L6

Barcelona (pop. 11,900) A clean and sparkling seaside resort of narrow streets and palm-shaded promenade, Sitges has the **Cau Ferrat Museum** (wrought ironwork, ceramics, pictures) in the house that belonged to the celebrated Catalan artist-author Santiago Rusiñol; the **Maricel Museum** (modern paintings by Catalan artists and 200 antique dolls); the **Romantic Museum** (furniture, decorations, musical instruments); and the **Santiago Rusiñol Library**.

Tarragona   L4

Tarragona (pop. 111,700) The foremost city of Roman Spain, Tarragona was founded by Publius Cornelius Scipio (237-183 BC), the greatest Roman general before Julius Caesar. The Emperor Augustus (63 BC-AD 14) lived here for two years. So for varying periods did Trajan (c.AD 53-117), Hadrian (76-138) and Antoninus Pius (86-161).

Many remains of Roman times have survived: several towers and substantial sections of defensive wall, some of it built on earlier (6th-century BC) Iberian walls whose massive stones can still be seen; the ruins of an **Amphitheatre** (*Anfiteatro*) in which Bishop Fructuoso and his deacons Augurio and Eulogio were martyred at the stake and in the centre of which a church was later built; the **Necropolis**, 3rd to 4th centuries AD, discovered when the tobacco factory was built on the site in 1952 (see the adjoining museum containing funerary urns and sarcophagi); the

Palace of Augustus, originally the Praetorium or residence of the Roman governor, later the palace of the kings of Aragón and Cataluña. Outside the town (3km/2mi) are the excellently-preserved **aqueduct** (*acueducto*) built by Trajan and known locally as the 'devil's bridge'; a Roman funerary monument, the so-called **Scipios' Tower** (*Torre de los Escipiones*), 6km/4mi along the road; and 20km/12mi along the road the **Arco de Bará**, a triumphal arch of the 2nd century AD.

The **Cathedral**, started in 1170, 52 years after the Moors were evicted from the town, has a striking statue of the Virgin Mary on the centre upright of its lovely main entrance, a solid marble font that is said to have been the Emperor Augustus' bath, altar steps made of stones from the Roman temple of Jupiter, a magnificent delicately-carved altar-piece of alabaster and cloisters formed by 276 marble columns with beautifully-carved capitals.

Tortosa N1

Tarragona (pop. 31,400) Near the delta of the River Ebro, Tortosa was founded by the 'Romans, occupied by the Visigoths, conquered in 714 by the Moors (who built the castle of La Zuda still to be seen above the town) and reconquered in 1148 by Christian forces under Ramón Berenguer IV, Count of Barcelona. The **Cathedral** was built on the site of a Roman temple during a period of exactly 200 years (1347-1547), though some additions were made in the early 18th century. Among its treasures are a 14th-century triptych of carved and painted wood, a retable from the workshop of the famous 15th-century Catalan craftsman Jaime Huguet and a baptismal font once part of a fountain in the castle-garden of the anti-pope Benedict XIII. (See **Peñíscola**.) His valuable silver chalice also used to be here but disappeared during the Civil War (1936-9). It was at Tortosa (24 July 1938) that the Republican forces crossed the Ebro to stop Franco's advance towards Valencia. This they did for four months at the shocking cost of 150,000 lives. See in Tortosa: the **Bishop's Palace** (*Palacio Episcopal*) and its lovely patio, built in the 14th century and in good repair; the **College of St Louis** (*Colegio de San Luis*), founded in 1544 as a school for young *moriscos* or Moors converted to the Christian faith; and **la Lonja**, built 1368-73, a simple, rectangular building of open arches, originally the town's exchange.

Ullastret H10

Girona (pop. 400) Here are important remains of a Greek village dating from 550-200 BC. It was discovered in 1947 on the hill called *Puig de Sant Andreu* and has houses, streets, drains, silos for grain storage, an acropolis and a museum full of superbly crafted pottery and jewellery.

Vic H7

Barcelona (pop. 30,100) Its vast **Cathedral** (11th-century bell-tower and crypt, 15th-century altar-piece and cloisters and the monumental tomb of the philosopher Jaime Balmes who was born here in 1810 and died here in 1848) has frescoes (including black and gold elephants) by the Catalan artist José María Sert (1876-1945) who also decorated the dining room walls in the Waldorf Astoria Hotel, New York. He painted the frescoes three times: 1900-15, 1926-30 (because he didn't like the originals) and finally after the cathedral was deliberately burned in 1936 and the priests murdered. Sert himself was buried in the cathedral at his own request.

In the **Episcopal Museum** is an important collection of paintings and polychromatic wood carvings, some dating back to the 11th century and mostly by Catalans – Ferrer Bassa, Pedro Serra, Bernard Martorell, Jaime Huguet and Lluis Borrassá.

Vilafranca del Penedès K5

Barcelona (pop. 25,000) Centre of the local wine industry. There is the **chapel of (San Juan)** founded in 1307 by the Knights of St John of Jerusalem and an interesting **Wine Museum** (*Museo del Vino*) containing a 4th-century BC wine press.

Vilanova i la Geltrú L6

Barcelona (pop. 43,600) An industrial town with important cotton-textile and other industries and a picturesque fishing quarter bordering its beach. This town has three things worth seeing: the **Castle** (*Castillo de la Geltrú*), a Catalan noble's dwelling, oldest building in the town and in excellent condition, with 12th-century surrounding wall and tower of homage, now used as an extension of the Balaguer Museum (see below); the **Casa Papiol** or house of the Papiol family, built 1790-1801 and preserved with its gas-lit reception, music, billiard rooms and its kitchen, oil and wine stores, stables and shady garden, an example of gracious living of 200 years ago; and the **Balaguer Museum and Library** (40,000 volumes) built in 1882 by the poet-politician Victor Balaguer (1824-1901) specially to house valuable articles including an Arab-Spanish bronze culinary mortar, a fine *Annunciation* by El Greco and paintings by the Catalan artist Mariano Fortuny (1839-74), El Greco's disciple Friar Maino (1568-1649), Escalante (1630-70) and Carreño (1614-85).

EXTREMADURA

Extremadura, comprising Spain's two largest provinces, is an inland region and has no coastline. It lies on the extreme west of the country and borders Portugal. To the north are the lovely Sierra de Gredos mountains where the almost extinct ibex can still be found, to the south another mountain range, the Sierra Morena.

Much of the land until recently was so poor and so neglected that all it produced was a crop once every eight or ten years. Now the huge 'Badajoz Plan', inaugurated by Franco in 1952, has brought 300,000 acres into cultivation, resettled 8000 families on holdings of 10-12 acres, established new towns and industries and built irrigation dams and reservoirs on the Guadiana.

Extremadura once formed part of Lusitania, one of the three provinces into which Roman Spain was divided and which also included central and southern Portugal. Its capital was the city of Mérida, still a rich treasure-house of Roman remains.

Local fiestas May 25-June 1: Cáceres. Fair and fiesta. Horse trials. Concerts. Bullfights. June 23-26: Coria (Cáceres). Each day a bull is let loose within the old walled town while the inhabitants dance and drink local punch until the bull interrupts the party. August 10-12: Miajadas (Cáceres). Popular fiesta and fair. August 15-20: Azuaga (Badajoz). Giants and dwarfs. Sports. Fireworks. Bullfights. Sept. 1-5: Mérida (Badajoz). Cattle fair. Bullfights. Oct. (1st week): Zafra (Badajoz). Machinery fair. Rounding up of cattle. Bullfights. Dec. 7: Torrejoncillo (Cáceres). Horsemen dressed in white accompany the Virgin to commemorate a victorious battle in the snow. Dancing.

Alcántara   E2

Cáceres (pop. 2300) Surrounded by walls 6m/20ft high, Alcántara is perched precariously on a rock over the River Tagus. It has the ruins of a **castle** in which the Order of the Knights of Alcántara was founded in 1146, a unique **Roman bridge** (40m/131ft high and the highest Roman bridge in Spain) built in AD 106 by Julio Lacer whose tomb is in the adjacent small temple; the 13th-century **Church of St Mary of Almozóvar**; the **Convent of St Benedict** (*San Benito*), built 1505-76.

Badajoz   I2

Badajoz (pop. 114,400) On the Portuguese border, Badajoz has a 13th-century fortress-like **cathedral** built on the foundations of a Moorish mosque; its tower and cloisters are 16th-century. Both the **alca**

zaba (castle) which dominates the town from a hill and the tower popularly known as the **Torre de Espantaperros** (the 'dog-scarer') were built by the Moors. The **Fine Arts Museum** (*Museo de Bellas Artes*) contains paintings by locally-born artists including Morales and Zurbarán.

Cáceres   F4

Cáceres (pop. 71,900) The *Qazrix* of the Moors and famous for ceramics and copperwork, this is a town of palaces, towers and arches. Among the **palaces**: *Sánchez-Paredes* (15th-century); *Pereros* (16th-century); *Las Veletas* (now a museum) on the site of the old *alcázar* or fortress, with escutcheons on its façade and a most interesting *algibe*, or underground water-storage system, 14 by 10m/46 by 33ft, built by the Moors; *La Cigüeña* with its 15th-century tower; the 16th-century *Casa del Sol* (House of the Sun); *Golfines de Abajo* with its very lovely façade and patio. Among **towers**: the *Torre de los Carvajal*, built by the Moors in the 13th century; the robust *Torre de Bujaco*; that of *los Púlpitos* ('the Pulpits'), 15th-century; *el Horno* ('the oven') and *la Hierba* ('the grass'), both Moorish; the *Torre Redonda* (the Round Tower), also Moorish; and the *Torre del Postigo* (the Postgate Tower), Moorish on Celtic and Roman base. Among **arches and gates**: *Arco de la Estrella* (Arch of the Star) built in the 18th century by José de Churriguera who was to give his name to the 'Churrigueresque' type of architecture; *Arco de Santa Ana* (Arch of St Anne); *Puerta de Mérida* (Mérida Gate); *Arco del Cristo* (Arch of Christ) and *Arco del Socorro* (Arch of Succour). Among **churches**: *San Mateo* (St Matthew), *Santiago* (St James), *San Juan* (St John) and *Santo Domingo*.

Coria   D4

Cáceres (pop. 10,400) The centre of a

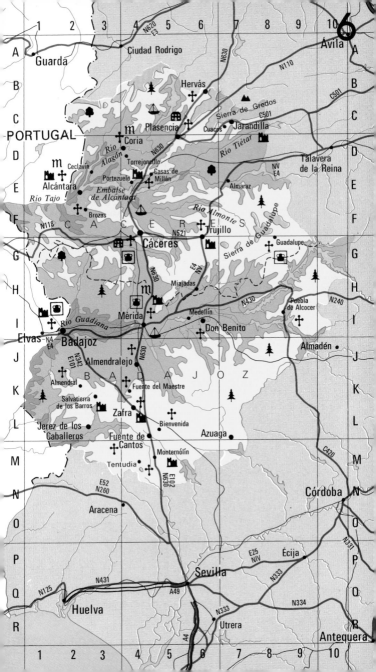

tobacco-growing district, Coria has sections of Roman granite walls, much repaired in the Middle Ages. The **Cathedral** has a single nave, lovely wrought iron screens, the tombs of bishops Pedro Jiménez de Prexamo and García de Galarza, and 14th-15th-century cloisters.

Guadalupe   G8

Cáceres (pop. 2800) Here is one of the most famous monasteries in Spain, founded in 1340 by Alfonso XI of Castile after his victory over the Moors. It was here the charter was signed for Columbus's expedition and here that the Indians who came back with him were baptized. Its famous wooden image of the Virgin (said to have been miraculously discovered by a cowherd in the 13th century) has been venerated by the Catholic Monarchs, the *Gran Capitán*, the Duke of Alba, Hernán Cortés, Cervantes and thousands of lesser mortals. Among its treasures are some very fine architecture including 15th- to 16th-century cloisters, a museum of miniatures, illuminated manuscripts, embroidery and eight paintings by Zurbarán.

Mérida   I4

Badajoz (pop. 41,900) The Roman Emerita Augusta, it abounds in Roman remains. It has a **Roman theatre** (*teatro romano*) built by Marcus Agrippa, son-in-law of Augustus, about 27 BC, seating 5500 and with a colonnaded stage 58m/190ft wide; an **amphitheatre** (*anfiteatro*), oval in plan, 126 by 102m/413 by 335ft, capacity 15,000; and the only Roman **circus** in Spain, capacity 30,000. It has a Roman **bridge** (800m/2625ft long, 60 arches) over the River Guadiana and another over the River Albarregas; two **aqueducts** – those of *San Lázaro* and *Los Milagros* ('the miracles', a name indicating amazement that the uniquely-balanced columns stand up); **Trajan's Arch** (*Arco de Trajano*); the **Temple of Diana** (*el Templo de Diana*); the remains of the **House of the Patrician** (*Casa Patricia*).

From Moorish times Mérida has the **Alcazaba** (Castle), built in 850 by Abderraman II of stone cut by the Romans, and the **Aljibe** (a large rainwater storage tank). See also the **Church of Santa Eulalia** (who was martyred in Mérida in 304) and the **Archaeological Museum** (*Museo Arqueológico*) containing much Roman statuary.

Plasencia   C5

Cáceres (pop. 32,200) Surrounded by 12th-century walls in which are six gates and 68 towers, Plasencia has an outstandingly beautiful 14th- to 16th-century **Cathedral** with an imposing doorway and innumerable artistic and architectural features in the interior. The retable is the work of Gregorio Hernández, the stalls were carved by Rodrigo Alemán in 1520 and there are also works by Diego de Siloé, Juan de Álava and Covarrubias. Surrounding the cathedral and the *Plaza de España* are the narrow, typically Spanish streets of the old town flanked by once-grand houses with balconies and wrought iron railings.

Trujillo   F6

Cáceres (pop. 9400) This was the birthplace of Francisco Pizarro (c. 1478-1541) whose unmarried mother abandoned him on the church steps. During his conquest of Peru he extorted the ransom of 'a roomful of gold as high as a man can reach with his sword' from the Inca chief Atahualpa, then had him strangled and was himself in due course murdered by the followers of Almagro whom Pizarro's brothers had also murdered. It was his brother Hernando, also born in Trujillo, who saved the Spanish exchequer from bankruptcy by bringing back from Peru vast quantities of gold. In the main square is a statue of Pizarro by the American sculptor Charles Carey Rumsey.

See the **Moorish castle**; the 16th-century **Convent of St Jerome** (*Convento de San Jerónimo*) where Francisco Pizarro was buried; **St Michael's Church** (*Iglesia de San Miguel*), founded by Queen Isabel I in the 15th century; **St Mary's Church** (*Iglesia de Santa María*) with its primitive retable of 25 panels painted by Fernando Gallegos; the 16th-century **St Martin's Church** (*Iglesia de San Martín*).

Zafra   L4

Badajoz (pop. 12,900) This was an Iberian, a Roman and a Moorish town. It has the imposing **Castle of the Dukes of Feria**, originally Moorish but rebuilt in the mid-18th century, with a superb patio and the famous *sala dorada* (gilded room). The castle is now a *parador*.

Roman Theatre, Mérida

CASTILLA-LA MANCHA

This vast area – 30,000sq mi/80,000sq km – produces much of the country's grain and wine and nearly all its saffron, the laboriously collected pollen of the purple crocus. The region comprises part of the high tableland of Castile and all the flat plain of La Mancha with its straight roads and wide horizons where Don Quixote tilted at the strange windmills just previously (1575) imported from Holland, then part of the Spanish empire. Here on the roofs of churches storks build their untidy nests, and buzzards (a metre long from beak to tail) are now permanent residents and no longer migratory.

Local fiestas Whitsun Sunday: Atienza (Guadalajara). Pilgrimage of muleteers in long capes and black hats, preceded by bagpipers, to local shrine. Dancing. Eating. Mule races. April (last Sunday): Mora (Toledo). Olive festival. Parade of decorated vehicles. Regional dancing. Handicrafts and cattle fair. Sept. (1st and 3rd Sundays): Mota de Cuervo (Cuenca). Collecting image of Virgin from hermitage and returning it (fortnight later) both journeys at rapid walk (6km/4mi in 32 mins). Sept. 2-8: Valdepeñas (Ciudad Real). Wine harvest festival. Important agricultural fair on permanent exhibition site. Processions. Dancing. Sports. Bullfights.

Albacete   *map 10*, **F3**

Albacete (pop. 117,000) Takes its name from the Moorish *al Basiti* and is widely known for its knives and scissors and the many bullfighters it produces. It is surrounded by the rich agricultural plain of La Mancha of Don Quixote fame. During the Civil War (1936-9) it was a headquarters for the International Brigades. It has a picturesque old quarter, *Alta de la Vila*. The 16th-century **Church of St John the Baptist** (*San Juan Bautista*) houses the image of the Virgin of the Plains which is carried through the streets on festive occasions.

Alcaraz   *map 10*, **H1**

Albacete (pop. 1800) A picturesque town of steeply-sloping streets. Alcaraz has the remains of two **Roman bridges** and of a **Moorish castle**, an attractive main square (*plaza mayor*); the **Aduana** (formerly the customs house, now the town hall) with a magnificent doorway; the 17th-century **Trinity Church** (*Iglesia de la Trinidad*) and the **Franciscan Church** containing

images by Salzillo and his talented pupil Roque López.

Almagro   *map 7*, **N7**

Ciudad Real (pop. 8400) A town of many escutcheoned houses dating from 16th and 17th centuries, Almagro is remarkable for two things. It was the birthplace in 1485 of Diego Almagro who conquered parts of Chile and Peru, made war against his countryman Pizarro and was executed by Pizarro's sons. It also has a unique **Corral de Comedias**, or 17th-century theatre, built around a courtyard.

Almansa   *map 10*, **G6**

Albacete (pop. 20,300) Clustering around the picturesque ruins of a 16th-century castle on a hill, Almansa belonged to the Knights Templar in the 12th to 13th centuries. It was the scene of the great battle (25 April 1707) between 34,000 men of Philip V, commanded by the British-born, French-naturalized Duke of Berwick, and 25,000 men of the pretender to the Spanish throne, Archduke Charles of Austria, commanded by the British general Lord Galloway, that marked the turning point in the War of Spanish Succession. The battle lasted three hours and in that time 9000 men died. See the **Casa Grande** (the Big House) with its magnificent porch and the 17th-century **Augustine Convent** (*Convento de las Monjas Agustinas*).

Atienza   *map 7*, **C11**

Guadalajara (pop. 1200) An enchantingly fascinating town whose centre is preserved as a national monument, while its ancient walls and fabulously-sited castle (only the tower of homage remains) are falling down. Atienza has seven churches (badly damaged in the Civil War), one of which, Holy Trinity, claims to possess a thorn from the crown of Christ.

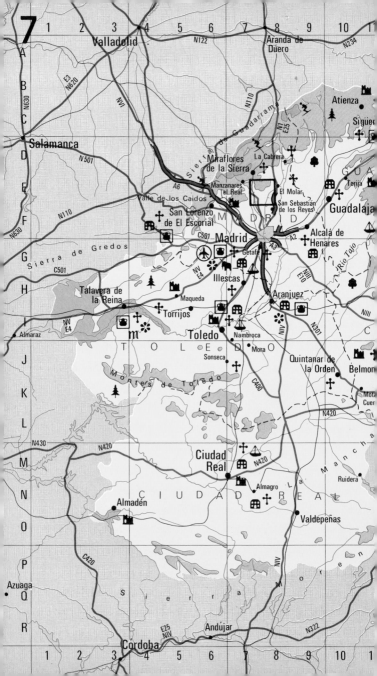

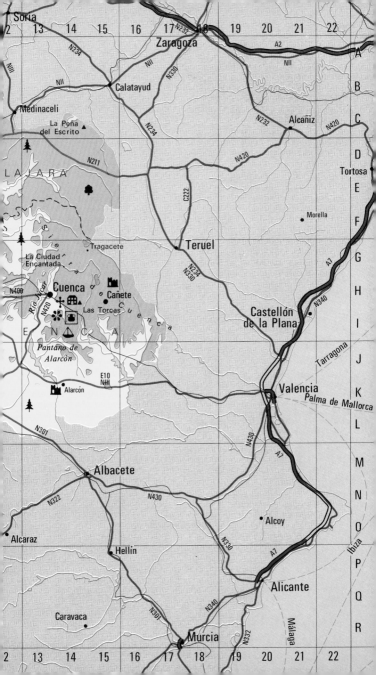

Ciudad Real   *map* 7, **M6**

Ciudad Real (pop. 51,100) This is known as the town of *pan y vino*, bread and wine, products of the surrounding plain of La Mancha, also prolific in partridges. Its name means 'royal city'. It was founded by Alfonso the Learned, King of Castile, in 1255 as a precaution against the mounting power of the Knights Templar and Knights of Calatrava. He surrounded it with walls and 120 towers, all of which have disappeared. The **Toledo Gate** (*Puerta de Toledo*), built by Alfonso XI in 1328 as one of the towers of the old *Alcázar* (castle) still remains. The oldest church is that of **St James**, but of greater architectural interest is the 14th- to 15th-century **Church of St Peter** (*San Pedro*). The brick-built **Cathedral** (1531-80), last altered in the 19th century when a new tower was added, has a rose window illuminating its huge single nave and a notable reredos by Giraldo de Merlo and his son-in-law Juan Hasten. 9km/5mi SE. of Ciudad Real are the remains of the old castle of **Calatrava la Vieja** where in 1164 San Raimundo de Fitero founded the military order of Calatrava whose headquarters were in 1217 transferred to the castle of **Calatrava la Nueva**, 3km/2mi from Calzada de Calatrava.

Cuenca   *map* 7, **H13**

Cuenca (pop. 41,800) The town was part of the dowry of the Moorish princess Zaida when she married the Christian king Alfonso VI of Castile and León in 1091, though the Moors retook it in 1108, killing her only son in the process. It was the birthplace of Alonso de Ojeda, discoverer of Venezuela. It was occupied by 2000 British and Portuguese troops in 1706 during the War of Spanish Succession. It is remarkable for its **casas colgadas**, or 'hanging houses', perched precariously on the precipitous hill with the Rivers Júcar and Huécar below. The 13th-century **Cathedral**, resembling a Norman church in Britain more than any church in Spain, has outstanding wrought ironwork, an altar by Ventura Rodríguez, a *Dolorosa* by Pedro de Mena, two paintings by El Greco and a unique 13th-century diptych.

18km/11miE. are **Las Torcas**, a group of remarkable crater-like depressions with jagged rims, the biggest, *la Torca del Lobo* (the Crater of the Wolf) being 170m/558ft in diameter. **La Ciudad Encantada** (Enchanted City) is 33km/20mi NE., a geological freak (covering 19½ sq km/7½ sq mi) of rock formations resembling buildings, streets, boats, faces, animals, huge mushrooms, even a swordfish fighting an elephant!

Guadalajara   *map* 7, **E10**

Guadalajara (pop. 57,000) Its foremost building is the **Palace of the Dukes of Infantado** (*Palacio de los Infantado*), built by the second duke, Íñigo López de Mendoza (1398-1458). In it (1559) Philip II, having failed to secure the hand of England's Elizabeth I, celebrated his betrothal to his third wife Elizabeth of Valois; Philip V was betrothed (1714) to Elizabeth Farnese; and Victor Hugo, then a child, stayed (1811) with his father, a Napoleonic general of the Peninsular War. The building, which has a magnificent façade, was severely burned in the Civil War but has been carefully restored. See also the **Church of San Ginés**, once part of the Dominican convent founded by Pedro Hurtado de Mendoza, and the 14th-century **Church of Santiago**.

Sigüenza   *map* 7, **C11**

Guadalajara (pop. 5700) Surrounded by the remains of walls and towers and with a picturesque main square, Sigüenza has a 12th- to 14th-century **Cathedral** (badly damaged 1936-9) containing a painting, the *Annunciation*, by El Greco, a chapel commemorating St Librana and her eight sisters, all of whom were martyred, and one of the best examples of sepulchral art in Spain – the reclining figure of the young warrior *El Doncel*, depicted reading a book.

Talavera de la Reina   *map* 7, **H3**

Toledo (pop. 64,100) Here the famous matador Gallito, the first bullfighter in history to fight 100 *corridas* in a single season, was at last fatally gored in 1920 at the age of 25. The town has an important ceramics industry, the remains of Roman and Moorish towers and walls, the 13th- to 15th-century **Church of St Mary** (*Iglesia de Santa María*) and the **Sanctuary of the Vírgen del Prado**, containing a collection of tiles made locally over the centuries.

Toledo   *map* 7, **I6**

Toledo (pop 57,800) Built on an eminence in a great curve of the River Tagus, this is one of the most historic places in the country. It was the capital of Visigoth Spain 569-712 and, after the Moorish occupation, capital of Catholic Spain 1085-1561. It is famous for its swords, its gold inlaid 'damascening' introduced by the Moors but today called 'Toledo Work' – and El Greco, who lived here for 39 years until his death in 1614.

The **Cathedral**, one of the biggest and loveliest in Spain, built 1226-1492, 111m/364ft long, 55m/180ft wide, has 88 pillars, 22 chapels, 750 stained-glass windows. The bell in its slender tower (90m/295ft) weighs 17½ tons. The huge 16th-century silver-gilt monstrance, fashioned by Juan de Arfe, is 2m/6ft high and weighs 230kg/507lb. El Greco's magnificent paintings of the apostles are here too. The other important Gothic building in Toledo is the 15th-century **Church of San Juan de los Reyes** which has an original cloister nicely restored, an octagonal cupola and much sculpted decoration by Juan Guas. The 10th-century **Church of the Christ of Light** (*Iglesia del Cristo de la Luz*), formerly a mosque built over Visigoth foundations, is Toledo's only intact Moorish building.

The massive Alcázar or fortress was pounded to rubble in the early days of the Civil War, after its defender, General Moscardó, had refused an ultimatum from the Workers' Militia for surrender within ten minutes or his son, in their hands, would be executed, a threat that was duly carried out.

In the 12th to 14th centuries, when Toledo had a large and influential Jewish community, living in amity with Christians and Muslims under such tolerant monarchs as Ferdinand III and Alfonso the Learned, there were eight synagogues. Two still exist: the truly magnificent **Santa María la Blanca**, with Moorish

capitals and arches, and **El Tránsito**, built in the 14th century by Pedro the Cruel's treasurer, Samuel Levi, a few years before the great Jewish massacre instigated by Pedro's rivals, the Trastamars, in 1355.

The **Hospital of the Holy Cross** (*Hospital de la Santa Cruz*), founded by the celebrated Cardinal Mendoza (1428-95) and now a museum, is decorated with Moorish tiles (*azulejos*) and contains 30 superb Brussels tapestries, two paintings by Ribera, one Goya and 18 El Greco's.

A tremendous amount of El Greco's work has been retained in Toledo. You can see it in the **House of El Greco** where, despite what you may be told, El Greco never lived: his house was nearby and has disappeared; the **El Greco Museum** (see the wonderful *View of Toledo*); the **Church of St Thomas** (*Iglesia de Santo Tomé*) containing his crowning masterpiece, the *Burial of the Count of Orgaz* with El Greco himself portrayed among the mourners; the **Church of Santo Domingo** (nine early works); the **Hospital of Tavera** (five later works and a small sculpture). El Greco's illegitimate son, Jorge Manuel Theotocopuli (El Greco lived with Jerónima Cubas but never married her) was architect of the Town Hall (*Ayuntamiento*).

MADRID

Alcalá de Henares   F9

Madrid (pop 142,900) This was the birthplace in 1547 of Spain's greatest writer, Miguel de Cervantes, author of *Don Quixote*, who died on the same day as Shakespeare (23 April 1616). It also owes its renown to the great **university** founded by the much-respected Cardinal Cisneros, one-time regent and inquisitor-general, in 1500. Although the university was transferred to Madrid in 1836 its lovely buildings (with 15 charming patios) still exist. The **Archbishop's Palace** (*Palacio del Arzobispo*), parts of which date to the 13th century (it was built by Archbishop Rodrigo Jiménez in 1209), contains the famous *Salón de Concilios*, the hall in which parliament met in 1348, and a large painting of the battle of Lepanto. Of the 38 churches, 21 convents and 27 other religious houses the town is said once to have possessed, few remain. But see: the **Magistral Church**, built 1139, enlarged 1498 by Cisneros (whose tomb it contains) on the site of the martyrdom (which a fresco depicts) of the child-saints Justo and Pastor in 304; the **Church of Santa María la Mayor** in whose parish register the baptism of Cervantes is recorded.

Aranjuez   H8

Madrid (pop. 35,900) Noted for strawberries, asparagus and its superb **Royal Palace** (*Palacio Real*). The palace (like the Escorial) was built by Juan Bautista de Toledo and Juan de Herrera. Work started in the reign of Emperor Charles V and finished in that of his son Philip II (1584). Damaged by fire several times, it was restored or enlarged by Philip V (who installed the monumental staircase) and by Ferdinand VI. There are many lovely rooms including the dining-rooms, the queen's boudoir, the throne room, the

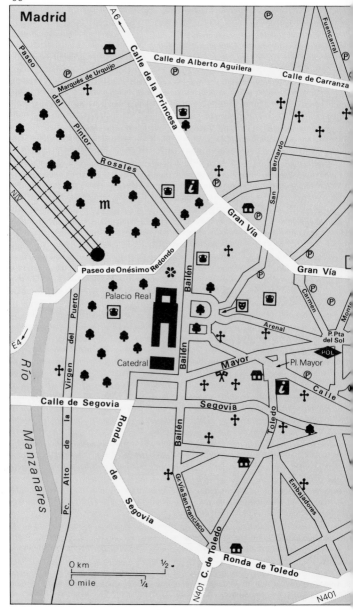

Madrid

A 6

Calle de Alberto Aguilera

Calle de Carranza

Paseo del Pintor Rosales

Marqués de Urquijo

Calle de la Princesa

Fuencarral

San Bernardo

N IV

Gran Vía

Gran Vía

Paseo de Onésimo Redondo

Carmen

Bailén

Palacio Real

Arenal

P. Pta del Sol

Virgen del Puerto

Monte

Río

Mayor

Pl. Mayor

POL

Catedral

Bailén

Calle

Manzanares

Calle de Segovia

Segovia

Toledo

Pc. Alto de la

Ronda de Segovia

Bailén

Gr. Vía San Francisco

Embajadores

0 km   ½

0 mile   ¼

N401 C. de Toledo

Ronda de Toledo

N401

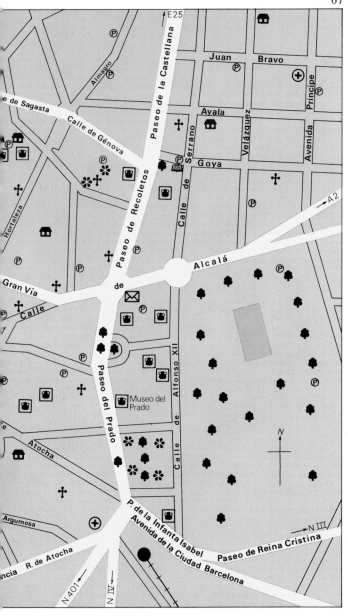

room of the ambassadors, the Arabian room, the *saleta* containing six canvases by Giordano, the Japanese room completely covered with porcelain and another room completely covered with mirrors. The gardens, with statues, fountains and a cascade beside the River Tajo, are as famous as the palace itself. In them is the **Casita del Labrador** (the Labourer's Cottage), in fact another palace that was the residence of the heir to the throne.

Escorial   F6

Madrid (pop. 9500) San Lorenzo de El Escorial is famous for the huge, austere palace-monastery of Philip II. The edifice covers eight acres, has 300 rooms, 2673 windows, 1200 doors, 86 staircases, 16 courtyards, 15 cloisters and nine towers. It houses 1600 paintings and murals. It has been called, with some justification, the eighth wonder of the world. It took 1500 workmen 21 years to build (1563-84) and although designed originally by Juan Bautista de Toledo was mainly the creation of Juan de Herrera. Philip II watched the progress of the work from a hillside seat 7km/4mi away. The impressive **Basilica**, approached through the *Patio de los Reyes* (Courtyard of the Kings), has retables painted by Navarrete, Urbina, Sánchez Coello, Carvajal and Cambiaso, sculptured monuments of Philip II (who came here to die) and his father Emperor Charles V, Benvenuto Cellini's fine crucifix and paintings by El Greco, Ribera, Titian and Claudio Coello. In the **Royal Pantheon** are the tombs of kings and queens of Spain from Charles I (1517-56) onwards, with the exception of the Bourbons. In the **Chapter Halls** are paintings by Velázquez, El Greco, Ribera, Navarrete, Titian, Veronese and Tintoretto. In the **Library** are 45,000 books, manuscripts and the 11th-century *Codici Aureo* whose illumination necessitated 8kg/17½lb of pure gold. In the two **Palaces**, built later (18th century) by Charles III, are valuable tapestries based on cartoons and drawings by Goya, Teniers, Mengs and others, furniture, porcelain, clocks and frescoes depicting historic battles.

Madrid   F8

Madrid (pop. 3,188,300) The lovely city that has been Spain's capital since 1561 (except 1601-06 when the court was moved to Valladolid), is roughly at the country's geographical centre on a tableland 700m/2296ft above sea level. It is a prosperous city of wide avenues, spacious parks (especially the **Retiro** with its *rosaleda*, or rose garden, and one of the largest artificial lakes in existence), hotels, theatres, night-life, 1500 restaurants serving the best food that every province in Spain produces, narrow alleys with fascinating bars; the country's biggest bullring (with a **Bullfight Museum** attached) and the modern football stadium of *Real Madrid*. The city was a battleground throughout the Civil War and never conquered despite being attacked by four columns and, in General Queipo de Llano's famous phrase, having a 'fifth column' inside.

Its main arteries radiate from its busiest square the *Puerta del Sol*, named after the 'gate of the sun', the east gate of the city in the 16th century. In the fascinating alleyways around it are the bars and restaurants so typical of Madrid. The hub of the old city was the *Plaza Mayor*, scene of bullfights, jousting and, under the Inquisition, burnings at the stake. In the centre of it today is the impressive equestrian statue of Philip IV by Juan de Bolonia. Other famous landmarks are the *Plaza de Cibeles* with its statue of this goddess of fertility by Francisco Gutierrez; the *Puerta de Alcalá*, the old gateway on the route to Alcalá de Henares; the *Plaza de Neptuno* (statue of Neptune by Juan Pascual de Mena); and the *Plaza de Colón* (Columbus).

The justifiable pride of Madrid – and Spain – is the **Prado Museum** (*Museo del Prado*) whose wealth of paintings is probably the finest in the world. There is so much to see that several visits are absolutely essential. Housed in an 18th-century building designed by Juan de Villanueva and inaugurated in 1818 with 311 paintings from the royal collection, it now has over 3000 (and 4000 drawings, 400 sculptures) displayed in 94 rooms on three floors. Of the Flemish primitives it has works by Roger van der Weyden and Hans Memlinc. It has 36 works by Titian, many by Raphael, Veronese, Tintoretto, Rubens (including the *Three Graces*, said to be his three wives) and Van Dyck. Spanish art is superbly represented by Morales, Coello, El Greco (34 works including the famous *Adoration of the Shepherds* and the *Crucifixion*), Alonso Cano, Ribera, Ribalta, Murillo, Zurbarán and nearly half of all the canvases the great Velázquez ever painted, including the *Surrender of Breda* and *las Meninas* (the Ladies-in-Waiting), so fantastically life-like that it has been said the artist captured the very air. There are no fewer than 10 rooms full of Goyas (110 paintings, 484 drawings) including his memorable *Third of May*, showing the victims of the French firing squad, the *Family of Charles IV* and the two celebrated *Majas*, one dressed, one nude.

The **Royal Palace** (*Palacio Real*) was

built by Philip V on the site of the *alcázar*, the fortress-residence (destroyed by fire in 1734) of the kings of Castile. (Said Napoleon to brother Joseph, installed in the palace as king of Spain: 'You are better lodged than I am.') Worth seeing are the black and white marble staircase, the throne room with vaulted ceiling painted by Tiepolo in 1764; the banqueting hall adorned with Brussels tapestries, decorated by Mengs, curtains depicting scenes from *Don Quixote* and 8km/5mi of superb carpets; the rooms of Charles III, the bed-chamber of Ferdinand VII; the library of 100,000 volumes and 3000 manuscripts; the royal armoury; the museum of carriages and harness; the royal pharmacy; and the chapel.

See also the **Museums of Modern and Contemporary Art** (*Museo de Arte Moderno y Museo de Arte Contemporáneo*) both in the same building at Paseo Calvo Sotelo 20; the **Goya Museum and Pantheon** (*Museo-Panteón de Goya*) in the Hermitage of *San Antonio de la Florida* where Goya is buried and which is decorated with his frescoes; the **Church of St Francis the Great** (*Iglesia de San Francisco el Grande*) in the *plaza* of the same name, built in 1784, with a huge dome 32½m/107ft in diameter (bigger than those of Les Invalides and St Paul's) and containing paintings by Goya, Alonso Cano, Zurbarán and Velázquez; the **National Archaeological Muséum** (*Museo Arqueológico Nacional*) at Calle Serrano 13; the **National Museum of Decorative Art** (*Museo Nacional de Artes Decorativas*) in Calle Montalbán 12 which has 62 rooms of furniture, ceramics, lace, tapes-

tries; and nearby at Montalbán 2 the **Naval Museum** (*Museo Naval*); the 17th-century **Cathedral** (*Catedral de San Isidro*) built by Francisco Bautista, main altar by Ventura Rodríguez, with tomb of St Isidro, patron saint of Madrid; the 15th-century **Casa de los Lujanes** where the French king Francis I was held prisoner after the battle of Pavia 1525; the **Convent of the Barefoot Carmelites** (*Convento de las Descalzas Reales*), a 16th-century building with a museum of paintings, sculptures, tapestries; the **Church of St Nicolas** (*Iglesia de San Nicolás*) with its *mudéjar* tower (built by Moslems who stayed after the Christian conquest), one of the oldest pieces of architecture in Madrid; the **Rastro** (open-air market).

Valle de los Caidos   E6

Madrid This is the fantastic monument to the dead of the Civil War (1936-9). The site was chosen personally by General Franco (who was himself buried there 1975). The huge subterranean basilica, hewn out of solid rock, is 247m/810ft long, has a tiled cupola 40m/131ft in diameter, a high altar bearing a statue of Christ by Veovide, pupil of Zuloaga, with the tomb of José Antonio Primo de Rivera, founder of the Falange movement and himself executed in the early months of the Civil War, in front of it. Above ground is a gigantic cross 148m/485ft high, 45½m/149ft wide, weighing 202 tons. Its black marble base bears sculptures 20m/66ft high by Juan de Ávalos of Matthew, Mark, Luke and John and representations of the four cardinal virtues – justice, prudence, fortitude, temperance.

Toledo

COMUNIDAD VALENCIANA

This region of three provinces is a 500km/ 311mi long Mediterranean coastal strip, never more than 120km/74mi wide and averaging only 70km/43mi. The southern part of its coast is the Costa Blanca, the White Coast, a modern touristic appellation suggested more than 2000 years ago by the Carthaginians who called the cliffs of Alicante *Acra Leuca*, or the White Fortress, and by the Romans who named the town *Lucentum*, the City of Light.

The Costa Blanca in summer is hotter than any other coastal part of Spain. This is where the almonds grow to make *turrón* (see **Food**), along with sizal and locust beans, about the only things, apart from early tomatoes where there is water, the soil of Alicante is capable of producing. Nevertheless the province is the centre of Spain's footwear industry, the factories of Elda and Elche exporting millions of pairs of shoes, mostly to the USA.

The northern part of the region – the provinces of Valencia and Castellón – could hardly be more different. Here the coastline is known as the Costa del Azahar, the Orange Blossom Coast, where the vast, orderly, deep-green orange groves bloom in the spring and give two million tons of fruit in the winter months of November through to March. Here too are the paddy fields producing rice for Spain's national dish *paella* (see **Food**). Most of them have been irrigated since the 13th century from the fresh water lagoon (largest in Spain) called La Albufera, haunt of eels and wading birds. **Local fiestas** January 1-5: Bocairent (Valencia). Mock battles between Moors and Christians in dress of period. Third Sunday in Lent: Castelló-Castellón. Picturesque pilgrimage to local shrine and return after dark. March 12-19: Valencia. *Las fallas.* Huge, artistic, mostly satirical tableaux (*ninots*) are displayed in the streets during week and burned on night of 19th. Fireworks. Bands. Processions in regional dress. Bullfights. End April: Alcoy (Alicante). Processions and realistic battles between Moors and Christians. June 21-29: Alicante. Processions. Bonfires. Election of Bonfire queen. Fireworks. Regional dances. Bullfights. July 25-31: Villajoyosa (Alicante). Battles between Moors and Christians on land and sea. August 13-15: Elche (Alicante). *The Mystery of Elche*, religious play with a continuous history since 13th century performed *in mid-air* inside dome of

church. End August-early Sept: Requena (Valencia). Wine festival.

Alcoy   L4

Alicante (pop. 65,900) A clean town of much industry. Alcoy was fortified by the Visigoth king Theodoric (420-51), victor over Attila the Hun in the battle of Chalons-sur-Marne. During the Moorish siege of 1276 the miraculous intervention of the town's patron saint, St George, is said to have turned the tide of battle. Many mementoes of the occurrence (paintings, statues and what is claimed to be an authentic hand of the saint in an elaborate reliquary) are in the modern church **Iglesia de San Jorge**. Other mementoes are in the **Casal de Sant Jordi**, named thus in *valenciano*, the local language almost identical to Catalan, and meaning the House of St George.

Alicante   N4

Alicante (pop. 251,400) Founded by the Carthaginians under Hamilcar Barca in the 3rd century BC, this is today the sophisticated centre of the Costa Blanca. It has a flourishing seaport and an international airport. Its palm-shaded promenade, whose paving of 7,000,000 curved tiles gives the illusion of undulation and induces a sailor's roll, is one of the prettiest in Spain. The **Castle of St Barbara** (*Castillo de Santa Bárbara*), in a majestic position atop the hill of Benacantil (200m/656ft), is in the main 16th- to 18th-century, though some traces of Moorish work are visible. **The Castle of St Ferdinand** (*Castillo de San Fernando*), in the municipal park, was built during the Peninsular War. It has two castles. The

The **cathedral** (*Catedral de San Nicolás de Bari*), built 1616-62, badly damaged by extremists in 1936 but later restored, has several good altar-pieces and sculptures. The 14th-century **Church of St Mary** was

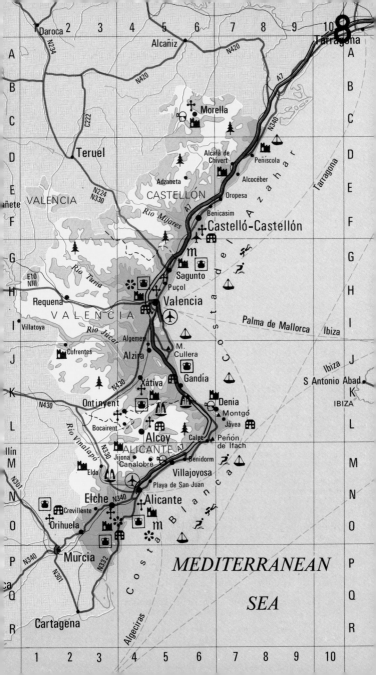

built on the site of a mosque, part of which remains. In the **Town Hall** (*Casas Consistoriales*) is the sea-level datum point from which all heights in Spain are measured. See also the **Provincial Museum** (*Museo Provincial*) which contains many objects found in the nearby Roman settlement of *Lucentum*; and **José Antonio's Prison** (now used as a youth hostel) where the founder of the Falange movement was tried and executed in the early months of the Civil War (1936-9). 5km/3mi outside the town the **Convent of the Holy Face** (*Convento de la Santa Faz*) possesses what is claimed to be a napkin with which St Veronica wiped the brow of Christ, and which bears the imprint of his face.

Calpe   L6
Alicante (pop. 8000) Calpe, whose rock the *Peñón de Ifach* (300m/984ft high and resembling Gibraltar) is almost completely surrounded by the sea, was utterly deserted for nearly 100 years after Algerian pirates in the 17th century put to the sword all the men and older women and carried off the younger women and children of both sexes for sale to North African brothels and harems.

Canalobre, Cave of   M5
Alicante Situated 1000m/3280ft above sea level in the *Cabeza d'Or* (Golden Peak) mountain, it has electrically-lit stalactites and stalagmites and is used for concerts and folk dancing in summer.

Castelló-Castellón   F6
Castellón (pop. 126,500) There is a port (6km/4mi distant) from which are shipped oranges, lemons and *carob* ('locust beans') grown on the surrounding plains and mountains. The **Capuchin Convent** (*Convento de las Capuchinas*) contains ten paintings on wood by Zurbarán. The interesting **Torre Mayor** or bell-tower which stands in the main square was built in 1519 of granite brought from Mallorca. Among the churches: **St Mary's** (*Santa María*) in the *Plaza de España*, **St Augustine's** (*San Agustín*), 14th-century, enlarged in 1650, with reredos by Vergara, and the 13th-century **St Nicholas** (*San Nicolás*). All three were severely damaged during the Civil War (1936-9).

Denia   K7
Alicante (pop. 22,200) A Greek colony 600 years BC, refuge of the Roman general Sertorius (see **Huesca**) in 85 BC, a bishopric in Visigoth times, capital of a kingdom and with a population of 50,000 under the Moors, Denia has the remains of **Iberian Settlements** *Coll de Pons* and *Penya de Águila*, a **Moorish Castle** and

several interesting caves including *la Cueva del Agua* 400m/1312ft up on *Montgó* mountain and containing two lakes.

Elche   N3
Alicante (pop. 162,900) Elche has footwear and textile industries, the largest forest of date palms in Europe (100,000 trees, some 30m/98ft tall, still irrigated by the system the Moors built and supplying the whole of Spain with palm fronds for the Holy Week processions) and the rich archaeological site of **La Alcudia** where the world-famous Iberian or possibly Greek carving, the *Dama de Elche*, was found. See the **Alcázar** (or castle but also known as the *Palacio de Altamira*); **La Calahorra** originally one of the towers that guarded the entrance to the town; the 18th-century '**Calendura**' Clock whose two carved figures strike the bell every quarter-hour; the **Church of St Mary** (*Iglesia de Santa María*) where the unique religious play, the *Mystery of Elche*, is performed *in mid-air*; the lovely **Convent of Mercy** (*Convento de la Merced*), built 1564; and the **Priest's Garden** (*Huerta del Cura*) with its 'imperial palm tree' of eight branches.

Gandía   K6
Valencia (pop. 48,500) This town has historical associations with the Borgia family who were made dukes of Gandía by Ferdinand II of Aragón in 1485. See the 16th- to 17th-century **Palace** (*Palacio del Duque de Gandía*) used today both as a museum and a sanctuary in memory of the more reputable Borgia, St Francis.

Játiva see Xátiva p. 74
Jijona   M4
Alicante (pop. 8,800) This is the home of the sweetmeat *turrón jijona* (see **Food**) and has the remains of a Moorish castle.

Morella   C6
Castellón (pop. 3300) Famous for the battle (1084) in which *El Cid* was defeated by the combined armies of King Sancho of Aragón and the Moorish king of Lleida, (Lérida), Morella has much of its medieval wall and castle still standing. The 13th-century **Church of St Mary** (*Iglesia de Santa María*) has two fine gateways – the Gate of the Apostles and the Gate of the Virgins. Nearby is the prehistoric cave *la Cueva de la Valle* containing wall paintings.

Orihuela   O2
Alicante (pop. 49,900) Where esparto mats are made and date palms grow. Orihuela has a 14th- to 15th-century **Cathedral** with an interesting 'doorway of

Alicante

chains' and a small museum (entry through the cloister) containing a Veláz-quez painting *The Temptation of St Tho-mas*; the **Church of St James the Apostle** (*Iglesia de Santiago Apóstol*) with a 15th-century tower and sculptures by Francisco Salzillo; the **Old University** (*Antigua Uni-versidad*), now a secondary school, with two 13th-century cloisters.

Peñíscola   D8

Castellón (pop. 3000) Built picturesquely on a rock almost completely surrounded by the sea, Peñíscola has a severe but imposing 14th-century castle founded by the Knights Templar in which the Spanish pope (or anti-pope) Benedict XIII (Pedro de Luna, chosen by the French cardinals in 1394 but recognized only by Spain and Scotland) took refuge in 1414 and stayed until his death ten years later, aged 94.

Sagunto   G5

Valencia (pop. 54,800) Famous for its heroic resistance to the siege of the Carthaginians led by Hannibal in 218 BC when the population eventually set fire to the town and threw themselves, men, women and children, into the flames rather than surrender. There are today the ruins of a **Roman Circus**, a **Roman Theatre** (capacity 8000), a **Temple to Diana** and of a huge **Castle** (part Roman, part Moorish and with later additions) built impressive-ly on a hill. A **Museum** contains many objects found in the town, some of them blackened by the fire over 2000 years ago.

Valencia   H5

Valencia (pop. 751,700) A city of gardens, oranges, rice and *paella*. Its vast *huerta* – 37,000 acres of it – is the most fertile plain in Spain. The city was destroyed by the Roman emperor Pompey in 75 BC, rebuilt by Sertorius, occupied by the Moors in 760, retaken by *El Cid* in 1094, lost in 1102 and finally held by the Christian forces under James I of Aragón and Cataluña in 1238. It was here, in 1474, that printing was first introduced into Spain.

The best building architecturally in Valencia is **la Lonja** (the Exchange), designed by Pere Compte, built 1483-9. Among the many treasures of the **Cathed-ral** (*la Seo*) are paintings by Goya, Ribera and Jacomart and goldsmith's work by Benvenuto Cellini. Also, the holy grail rescued by Joseph of Arimathea after the Last Supper and sought by King Arthur, Sir Galahad, Sir Launcelot, Parsifal, Lohengrin and a multitude of others in legend is claimed to be here in fact. It is of agate, with a jewel-encrusted base, and measures 17 by 16cm/6½ by 6in overall. The cathedral has three fine doorways – the Door of the Apostles (outside which every Thursday the 'water tribunal' meets to settle farmers' irrigation disputes), the Lleida (Lérida) Gate (so-named because seven married couples from Lleida are said to have been entrusted with the task of enticing from that town 700 maidens to help to repopulate Valencia quickly) and the door of the *Miguelete* in the octagonal tower of the same name (built 1381-1417, height and perimeter both 60m/196ft) from the top of which there is an impressive view of the city. Next to the cathedral is the 17th-century **Basilica of the Madonna of the Forsaken** (*Basílica de Nuestra Señora de los Desamparados*), notable for frescoes by Palomino.

See also in Valencia: the **Palacio del Marqués de Dos Aguas** with its ornate 'churrigueresque' façade designed by Hipolita Rovira who died insane, and now housing the **Ceramics Museum**; the **Church of St Stephen** (*Iglesia de San Esteban*) where the daughters of *El Cid* were married and the saint Vicente Ferrer baptized; the **Church of Santos Juanes**, 14th-century, façade 1900, ceiling of dome painted in 1700 by Palomino (who also designed the frescoes on the ceilings of the churches of St Martin and St Nicholas, although they were actually painted by Dionisio Vidal); the **Church of St Catherine** (*Iglesia de Santa Catalina*) with its hexagonal tower; the **Towers of Serranos**, built by Pedro Balaguer in 1393; the **Towers of Cuarte**, 15th-century; the **Pro-** vincial **Museum of Fine Arts** (*Museo Provincial de Bellas Artes*) containing many important works of art; the **Museum of Bullfighting** (*Museo Taurino*).

Xàtiva K4

Valencia (pop. 23,800) Home of the Spanish branch of the Borgia family (which produced two popes – the remarkable Alexander VI who had eight illegitimate children, including Caesar and Lucrezia, by the Italian Beauty Vanozza, and the far more reputable Calixtus III) and birthplace of José de Ribera the painter. Xàtiva gave Europe its first non-imported paper and the world its first shorthand (invented by Martí). A fascinating town of narrow alleys and escutcheoned mansions, it has a **Moorish castle** and a **Moorish fountain** (still in use). See the **Church of St Felix**, 1596, which contains the tomb of Archbishop Juan Borgia; the 13th-century **Hermitage of St Felix**; and the **Fine Arts Museum** (*Museo de Bellas Artes*) in the 16th-century building known as *El Almudín*.

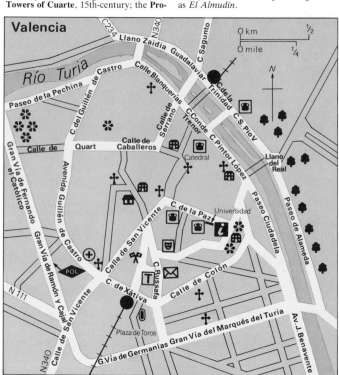

ANDALUCÍA

For many people Andalucía is the 'real Spain', the land of guitars and castanets, of swirling dresses and stamping feet as gipsies dance in caves, of donkeys and packmules padding softly through narrow, earthen streets, of dazzling white houses with cool, entrancing patios and wrought iron gates and grilles, of Arab horses and fighting bulls.

Not only is Andalucía the most fascinating of all Spain's regions, it is the second biggest. It has 450km/280mi of coast – the Costa del Sol or Sunny Coast, where sugar cane and custard apples grow – bordering the Mediterranean and 270km/168mi more – the Costa de la Luz or Coast of Light – washed by the Atlantic. Rising behind the Costa del Sol are the massive Snowy Mountains or Sierra Nevada where there are a genuine glacier (the most southerly in Europe), 100 lakes and lagoons and Europe's highest road 54km/33mi long. You can ski in the Sierra Nevada in the morning and bask in the sun of the Costa del Sol the same afternoon.

Flowing through the region almost from one side to the other is the River Guadalquivir and its tributaries. There are wide expanses of cereals dotted with typical Andalusian farmsteads called *cortijos*, thousands of acres of cotton, enormous olive groves of ancient gnarled trees. There are cork oaks around the Bay of Gibraltar, salt pans near Cádiz and groves of bitter Sevilla oranges whose entire crop goes into the marmalade on Britain's breakfast tables.

There is also industry – coal, iron, lead, the Río Tinto copper mines, shipbuilding, even aeroplane building. But more interesting to the visitor will be the great variety of Andalusian handicrafts – wrought ironwork, lace, pottery, tapestry, fans, *mantillas*, the esparto mats of Guadix, the leatherwork of Ubrique, the dolls and ceramics of Chiclana, the handwoven textiles of the Alpujarra mountains, the gold and silver work of Córdoba, and the *trajes de luces*, 'suits of lights', worn by matadors and made in Sevilla.

What helps to make Andalucía so fascinating is its rich cultural inheritance from the Moors. Of course the Romans were here too for 600 years (206 BC to AD 414). They built the *Vía Augusta*, the great road from Cádiz round the coast right to the Pyrenees. The Roman emperors Trajan, Hadrian (who built the massive wall to separate the English and the Scots) and Marcus Aurelius ('one of the noblest figures in all history') were all

Andalusians by birth, as were Seneca the philosopher, Mela the agriculturalist, Columella the geographer and his grandson Lucan the poet.

But the Moors were here even longer than the Romans and their fabulous architecture still takes the breath away after more than 1000 years. It was they, too, who brought to Spain the peach, the apricot, the pomegranate, the sugar cane, the medlar tree, rice and cotton. They founded textile industries – especially wool and silk (the city of Almería alone had 5000 looms) – made ceramics and carpets and laid out irrigation systems some of which are still in use.

It was the Moors who gave us our numerals and *algebra*, still known by that Arab word today; who in the 12th century introduced paper into Europe through their university at Córdoba and in the 13th century (at the Battle of Niebla, near Huelva) were the first to use gunpowder as a propellant.

It was the Moors also who, intermarrying with the native Spaniards, contributed the dusky tinge that still persists in the Andalusian complexions of today.

Local fiestas Mid-Feb. (seven days): Cádiz. Choir festival. Humorous processions. Masked dancing. Fireworks. Bullfighting. April 18-23 (though dependent upon Easter): Sevilla. The famous April fair. Non-stop gaiety in streets that are tunnels of coloured lights. By day, riders and señoritas mounted in pairs in Andalusian dress. By night, singing *flamenco* and dancing *sevillanas*. Bullfights. Cattle fair. April, last Friday, Saturday, Sunday: Andújar (Jaén). Massive pilgrimage (in regional dress and on horseback) to mountain shrine of Nuestra Señora de la Cabeza. Saturday: dancing all night. Early May (date varies): Jerez de la Frontera. Spring fair, second in importance only to that of Sevilla. Horse racing. Bullfights.

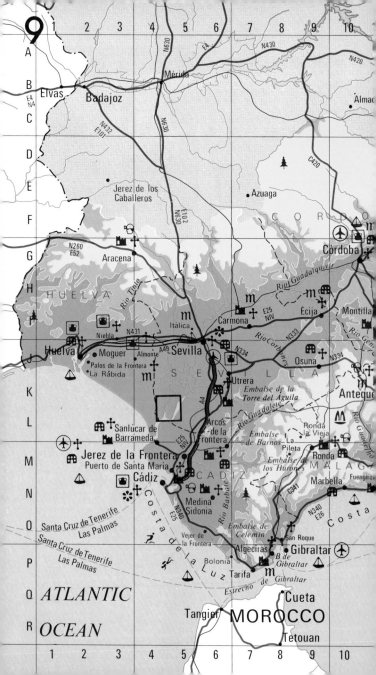

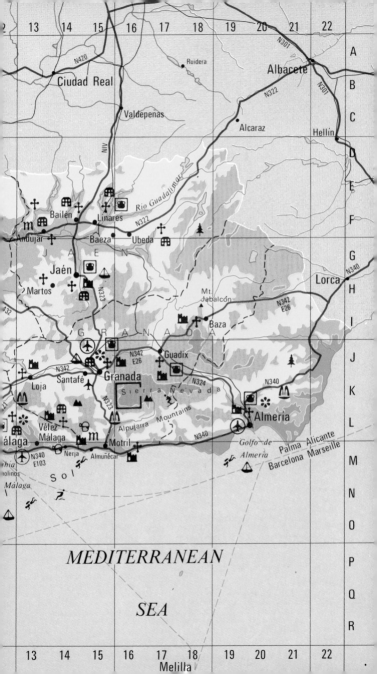

May 1-15: Córdoba. Competition for best-kept patio. *Flamenco* dancing. Processions of decorated vehicles. Horseriders in *cordobés* dress. Bullfights. Whitsun Saturday, Sunday, Monday: Almonte (Huelva). Thousands of pilgrims from whole of western Andalucía on foot, horseback and mulecarts in honour of Our Lady of the Dew. Solemn mass. *Flamenco* dancing. End August-early Sept (date varies): Montilla (Córdoba) Grape harvest festival. Early Sept (date varies): Jerez de la Frontera. Wine festival. Ceremonial treading of grapes. *Flamenco* dancing. Equestrian events. Bullfights.

Algeciras   P8

Cádiz (pop. 86,000) This busy port on the Bay of Gibraltar was a town in Roman times and a landing place for the Moors in 711 when they swarmed across the straits from North Africa to begin their 781 years' occupation of Spain. It has an **aqueduct** (built in 1784 and still bringing water to the town), the 18th-century **Church of Santa María de la Palma** and a famous British-owned hotel (now a Trust House).

Almería   L20

Almería (pop. 141,000) The Moors called it *Espejo del Mar* (Mirror of the Sea) and an earthquake destroyed it in 1522. Grapes, oranges and esparto grass are shipped from here and it shares in the tourist prosperity of the Costa del Sol. The town is dominated by the **Alcazaba** (Moorish castle) built by Abderraman III (912-61) and enlarged by his successors Almanzor and Hairan. Its tower of homage (*torre del homenaje*) was added by the Catholic Monarchs. The unusual **Cathedral**, built in 1524 to plans by Diego de Siloé, was also a fortress – to defend the town against pirates. The 18th-century altar-piece and choir stalls were carved by Juan de Orea. There are tapestries by Alonso Cano and an image by Salzillo. Among the churches: **Santo Domingo**, 17th-century, containing an image of the town's patron saint, the 'Virgin of the Sea', discovered on a nearby beach in 1502; **San Pedro** (St Peter), built 1795; and the **Monastery Church of the Immaculate Conception** (*Iglesia del Real Monasterio de la Purísima Concepción*) containing an image attributed to Alonso Cano.

Almuñécar   M16

Granada (pop. 16,100) The Old Roman settlement of *Sexi*, and one of the prettiest towns on the Costa del Sol, Almuñécar has an **aqueduct** and a burial tower **la Torre del Monje** (the Tower of the Monk), both of Roman origin, the remains of a

Moorish Castle and **la Cueva de los Siete Palacios**, a cave with seven vaulted chambers.

Andújar   F13

Jaén (pop. 35,000) An agricultural market town on the River Guadalquivir (over which there is a **Roman bridge**), Andújar was demolished and its inhabitants massacred as a reprisal for rebelling against their Roman masters. **St Mary's Church** (*Iglesia de Santa María*), 15th- to 16th-century, was built on the site of a mosque. 30km/19mi to the N. is the shrine of **la Virgen de la Cabeza**, famous in the Civil War for its heroic resistance to an eight month siege during which 22 babies were born and most of its defenders died.

Antequera   K11

Málaga (pop. 35,200) Here are the ruins of a **Moorish castle** with an interesting five-cornered 'tower of homage', several churches (among them **San Agustín** in which is the standard captured from the Moors by Rodrigo de Narváez), the **Convento de Monteagudo** whose tower is wider at the top than at the bottom, the **Convent of Belén** in which is Murillo's painting *The Adoration of the Shepherds*, the **Hospital of San Juan de Dios** (St John of God) whose 'arch of St Mary' is composed of inscribed tablets·from the nearby Roman settlements of *Singilia* and *Osone*. On the outskirts of the town are three dolmens: the almost world-famous **Menga Cava** enclosed by 15 huge blocks of stone, the adjoining **Viera Cave** dating from the Bronze Age and, 3km/2mi from the town, the **Romeral Cave**. 9km/5mi from Antequera is the much-visited geological freak of rocks in strange formations **El Torcal**.

Aracena   G3

Huelva (pop. 6300) Aracena has a 13th-century church **Iglesia del Castillo** built by the Knights Templar and the well-known **Gruta de las Maravillas** (the Grotto of the Marvels) with 12 'rooms' and six underground lakes.

Arcos de la Frontera   M6

Cádiz (pop. 25,000) This is one of the prettiest towns in Spain. It is perched on a ridge-shaped hilltop overlooking the valley of the Guadalete where the Moors decisively defeated the Visigoth King Roderick in 711. Its streets are clean, tortuous and enchantingly medieval. It has a **castle**, once the residence of Moorish kings and later of the counts of Arcos, several ducal palaces, three of the original town gates and the **Church of St Mary** with choir stalls carved by Diego Roldán.

Baeza F15

Jaén (pop. 14,800) Dominating a vast, fertile plain and once a Moorish capital which the Christians captured and lost several times in the 12th to 13th centuries, Baeza is a town of innumerable noble buildings. There are palaces (see the 15th-century **Palacio de Jabalquinto**); a **cathedral** containing magnificent wrought ironwork by the famous craftsman Bartolomé of Jaén; churches – see those of the **Holy Cross** (*Santa Cruz*), 13th-century; **San Pablo** (St Paul), 15th-century; **San Andrés** (St Andrew), early 16th-century; **Salvador** (Saviour), romanesque but much-restored; two imposing gateways (the **Jaén Gateway** and the **Villalar Arch**), both 16th-century and erected in honour of Emperor Charles V; a mid-15th-century **Town Hall** (*Ayuntamiento*); the **Old Meat Market** (*Antigua Carnicería*) now housing the municipal archives; an outstandingly attractive **Market Square** (*Plaza del Mercado*); the lovely 16th-century **Casa del Pópulo** now used as a tourist information office; and, nearby, the **Fountain of the Lions**, whose central statue is said to be of Himilce, Spanish wife of Hannibal.

Bailén F14

Jaén (pop. 15,600) This is an undistinguished town whose only real claim to fame is that here on 19 July 1808, during the Peninsular War, Napoleon's army received its first defeat, with 20,000 casualties and surrendered with all its arms.

Baza I18

Granada (pop. 20,600) Centre of mercury, lead and iron mining, Baza has the remains of an interesting **Moorish castle** (*Alcazaba*) on the slopes of Mount Jabalcón, and **St Mary's Church** (*Colegiata de Santa María*), formerly a cathedral, rebuilt 1529-61, tower added in the 18th century.

Cádiz N4

Cádiz (pop. 157,800) Built on an isthmus and one of Spain's biggest ports, Cádiz was founded by the Phoenicians about 1000 BC. It is the oldest town in the country but has few old buildings – chiefly because of destruction wrought by Drake (1587), Essex (1596) and Nelson (1797), but also because of a tidal wave (1755), Napoleon (1810) and an ammunition explosion (1947). Spanish mothers along this coast still threaten disobedient children that Drake, or *el Draque*, will come and take them.

But despite the catastrophes, some things remain: the **Cathedral**, 18th- to 19th-centuries, with paintings by Murillo and Zurbarán, sculptures by *La Roldana* and Martínez Montañez and the tomb of Manuel de Falla, the Cádiz-born composer; the 17th-century **Church of St Catharine** (*Iglesia de Santa Catalina*) containing Murillo's *Mystical Betrothal of St Catharine*, unfinished when the artist fell to his death from a scaffolding here; the elliptical **Church of St Philip Neri**, also with a Murillo painting; the subterranean **Church of the Holy Cave** (*Iglesia de la Santa Cueva*) which has three paintings by Goya; the **Women's Hospital** (*Hospital de Mujeres*) containing the famous *Ecstasy of St Francis* by El Greco; the **Museum of Paintings** (*Museo de Pinturas*) containing works by Murillo, Zurbarán and Van Dyck; and the **Archaeological Museum** (*Museo Arqueológico*).

Carmona I7

Sevilla (pop. 22,800) Carmona has a most important **Roman necropolis** of more than 900 tombs and funerary caskets dating from the 1st to 4th centuries AD, two **gates** (*Puerta de Sevilla* and *Puerta de Córdoba*), both Roman with Moorish additions, and the reconstructed **Moorish Castle** (*Alcazaba*). See also **St Mary's Church** (*Iglesia de Santa María*), its Moorish courtyard and 15th-century triptych.

Córdoba G10

Córdoba (pop. 284,700) World famous for its Moorish mosque, Córdoba is a town of great character and beauty. It enjoyed its greatest splendour under the Muslim emir Abderraman I (756-88). It is said to have had a million inhabitants and was the capital of an independent state. Today it is the centre of the cotton industry and renowned for the work of its silversmiths. Its old Jewish quarter (*Barrio de la Judería*) is a paradise of patios, squares, gardens, wrought iron gates and grilles.

The **Mosque** (*la Mezquita*) is one of the most beautiful buildings in the world and the only mosque (unfortunately, from the architectural point of view) with a Christian church built into it. It dates from the 8th century, was partly enlarged in the 10th century and has been a Christian cathedral since the city was captured from the Moors in 1236. Its veritable forest of marble, granite and jasper pillars (850 remain of the original 1000) gives it a breath-taking beauty. There are 19 aisles in one direction, 36 in the other. It has four lovely doorways, the famous *Patio de los Naranjos* (Court of the Orange Trees) with its fountains, several chapels, choir stalls of carved mahogany, images by Alonso Cano and Pedro de Mena, a retable by Berruguete, the tombs of the poets Luis de Góngora and Garcilaso de la

The Mosque, Córdoba

Vega and, among the valuable cathedral treasures, a monstrance by Juan de Arfe (1535-c. 1603) and a golden chalice by the Florentine craftsman Benvenuto Cellini (1500-71). For the story of the bells see **Santiago de Compostela**.

Near the mosque, in Calle Velázquez Bosco, is the **Cathedral Museum** (*Museo de la Mezquita-Catedral*), containing numerous objects found during restoration work over the centuries, and the **Arab Baths** (Baños Árabes). Not far away is the **Archaeological Museum** (*Museo Arqueológico*) containing a Neanderthal skull and the famous bronze stag found at Medina Azahara (9km/5mi distant), a palace (today in ruins but worth visiting) built by Abderraman II in 937 for his favourite concubine.

The **Fine Arts Museum** (*Museo de Bellas Artes*) in the lovely square *la Plaza del Potro* has paintings by Murillo, Zurbarán, Ribera and Valdés Leal and works by the famous Córdoban sculptor Mateo Inurria. In the same building (the Old Charity Hospital founded by the Catholic Monarchs and having one of the loveliest patios in Córdoba) is the **Museum of Julio Romera de Torres** devoted to the paintings of gipsies and bullfighters by this famous local artist. Other mementoes of bullfighters, especially of the Córdoban matadors *Lagartijo*, *Guerrita*, *Machaquito*, *El Cordobés* and the great *Manolete*, together with local leather and silverwork, are shown in the **Casa de las Bulas**. Those interested should also see, in the *Plaza del Conde de Priego*, Manolete's grandiose monument.

Among Córdoba's many churches (*iglesias*): **Santa María** in three styles of architecture and containing paintings by Castillo, sculptures by Gómez de Sandoval; **San Lorenzo** with baroque porch, octagonal tower and interesting roof and mural paintings; **San Pablo** containing a fine religious image of *Our Lady of the Sorrows* by Juan de Mena; the romanesque church of **La Magdalena**; **San Jacinto** whose façade is 15th-century; the 18th-century **San Nicolás** with octagonal tower and Renaissance façade; **San Hipolito**, a modern church containing monuments to Alfonso XI and Ferdinand IV, much silver treasure and a sculpture attributed to Pedro Roldán; the **Church of the Convent of Mercy** (*Iglesia Conventual de la Merced*) containing a huge baroque retable, a 13th-century Crucifixion and some fine cloisters; the lovely chapel (*capilla*) of **San Bartolomé** in the heart of the Jewish quarter and, in the same district, the 14th-century **Synagogue** where Maimónides the Jewish philosopher was born and second in importance only to that of Toledo.

Also worth seeing in Córdoba: the **Castle of the Christian Kings** (*Castillo de los Reyes Cristianos*), built in 1328; the **Palace of the Marquises of Viana** (*Palacio de los Marqueses de Viana*) which has 14 lovely patios; the Moorish tower known as **La Calahorra**; the **Puente Romano** or Roman Bridge and the remains of the Moorish watermills at the riverside nearby; the **Torre de la Malmuerta** (1406); and the **Zoco** used for the sale of handicrafts by day and *flamenco* dancing at night.

Écija   I9

Sevilla (pop. 34,600) There are ancient walls and noble houses and its bullring is built over a Roman amphitheatre. Among the churches, **St James** (*Santiago*) has a pleasant, recently-restored 18th-century patio; **Our Lady of Mercy** (*Nuestra Señora de la Merced*) contains sculptures by Martínez Montañés; and **Holy Cross** (*Santa Cruz*) has a Moorish tower and 7th- to 8th-century Christian coffins.

Fuengirola   N11

Málaga (pop. 30,600) A picturesque resort which has the remains of a **Moorish Castle** built by Abderraman III in 956 where the Moorish philosopher Abderraman-ben-Abdallah was born.

Granada   J15

Granada (pop. 262,200) For 781 years centre of Moorish civilization until its reconquest by the Christians in 1492, Granada is today one of the show places of Europe. It lives from tourism and craftsmanship – carpets, embroidery, tapestries, *mantillas*, copperwork and leatherwork. It is built on twin hills – the

Albaicín, a district of entrancing patios, and the *Alhambra*, crowned by the Moorish palace-fortress of the same name.

The **Alhambra**, in whose gardens the nightingales sing, was built 1248-1350. In its heyday it had 30 towers, some of them veritable palaces. The Emperor Charles V (1517-56) destroyed some of them and built himself a palace there, an outstanding example of Renaissance architecture. Napoleon blew up eight more towers. In 1821 an earthquake destroyed some more. Even so, it is one of the most fabulous buildings in Spain, thanks largely to the writings of the American author Washington Irving (1783-1859) who lived amid the ruins and inspired Queen Isabel II to start restoration in 1862. Many of the halls, patios and towers have names that have become household words: the Court of the Myrtles (*Patio de las Arranyanes*) with its pool bordered with lovely arches; the Court of the Lions (*Patio de los Leones*) with its famous fountain supported by 12 carved lions and flanked by 124 marble pillars; the Hall of the Ambassadors (*Sala de Embajadores*), with walls decorated in geometric design; the Hall of the Two Sisters (*Sala de las Dos Hermanas*) with richly decorated walls and ceilings; the Room of Secrets (*Sala de los Secretos*) whose acoustics make whispers audible.

In the **Palace of Charles V** are the **Fine Arts Museum** (*Museo de Bellas Artes*) and the **Spanish-Moslem Museum** (*Museo Hispano-Musulmán*) containing a huge decorated vase and other local discoveries.

Adjoining the Alhambra is the **Alcazaba**, the castle which formed the outer defences. It has two famous towers – *la Torre de la Vela* whose bell sounded the alarm when danger threatened and *la Torre del Homenaje*, the Tower of Homage. Above and behind the Alhambra is the **Generalife**, the summer palace of the Moorish kings, finished in 1319, with delightful gardens and the cool and beautiful **Patio de la Acequia** (Court of the Running Water).

The **Cathedral** was designed by Diego de Siloé in 1528, consecrated in 1561, completed in 1703. The main front was

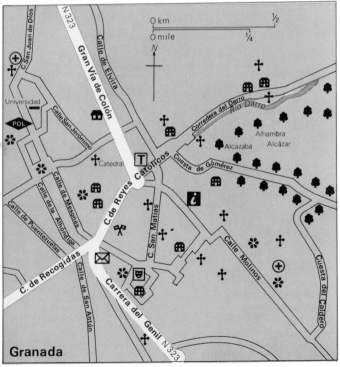

Granada

designed by Alonso Cano, many of whose sculptures adorn the interior. There are also paintings (some that belonged to the Catholic Monarchs) by Roger van der Weyden, Memlinc, Botticelli and others. In the sacristy are King Ferdinand's sword, Queen Isabel's crown and sceptre and a *Crucifixion* by Martínez Montañés. Adjoining the cathedral is the early-16th-century **Royal Chapel** (*Capilla Real*) designed by Enrique Egas, containing the kneeling figures (carved by Felipe de Vigarny) of the Catholic Monarchs, whose mausoleum and those of their daughter Joan the Mad and her husband Philip the Handsome are in the transept.

See also in Granada: the **Monastery of St Jerome** (*Monasterio de San Jerónimo*) founded in 1492, designed by Diego de Siloé and built by the Duchess of Sessa as a burial place for her husband, Gonzalo de Córdoba, the *Gran Capitán*; the 16th-century **Church of Santa Ana**; the 11th-century **Arab Baths** (*Bañuelo* or *Baños Árabes*); the **Casa del Castril**, a lovely 16th-century palace housing the **Archaeological Museum**; the **Law Courts** (*Audiencia*) in the 16th-century Chancellery (*Palacio de la Cancillería*); the **Casa de los Tiros**, an 11th-century Moorish nobleman's house with the sculptured figures of Hercules, Perseus, Mercury, Orion and Jason on its façade and a fine ceiling inside; the 16th-century monastery **La Cartuja** on the outskirts of the town; the **Alcaicería**, originally the Moorish silk market but today a group of 200 shops and stalls selling local handicrafts; and the **Caves of Sacromonte** where gipsies dance and sing *flamenco*.

Guadix   J17
Granada (pop. 19,900) A high proportion of the population lives in caves (with electric light, gaily-painted doors and oddly-shaped chimneys). Guadix has walls and towers built by the Moors, a lovely **Cathedral** designed by Diego de Siloé, started in the 16th century completed in the 18th, pulpit and choir stalls carved by Alonso Cano's pupil Ruiz del Peral; a **Cathedral Museum** containing embroidery by Queen Isabel I and the mummified arm of St Torcuato, first bishop of the diocese; and the ruins of the Moorish **Alcazaba** (Castle).

Huelva   J2
Huelva (pop. 127,800) Centre and port serving the Río Tinto mines, Huelva has a 17th-century **Cathedral Church** (*Iglesia Catedral de la Merced*) once part of a convent; **St Peter's Church** (*Iglesia de San Pedro*) built on the foundations of a mosque; the 16th-century **Church of the Conception** (*Iglesia de la Concepción*); the **Church of St Francis** (*Iglesia de San Francisco*) containing the sepulchre of the famous admiral Andrés de Vega Garrocho and works by Pacheco and Montañés; and the **Palace of the Dukes** that belonged to the Dukes of Medina Sidonia and the Counts of Niebla. There is also an **Archaeological Museum** (*Museo Arqueológico*) containing relics of Neolithic, Roman and Moorish times. On the outskirts of the town at *Punta del Sebo* is an imposing monument by the American V. Whitney commemorating Columbus' discovery of the New World.

Itálica, Ruins of   I5
Sevilla Itálica, founded originally as a rest camp for his troops by Publius Cornelius Scipio (237-183 BC), the greatest Roman general before Julius Caesar, developed into the most important Roman city in Bética (Andalucía). It was destroyed by the Moors in the 8th century but still visible today are the streets, mosaic floors, statues, amphitheatre (one of the biggest in the Roman Empire, capable of holding 25,000 people), the forum and several houses with hypocausts.

Jaén   H14
Jaén (pop. 96,400) A typical Andalusian town built on the slopes of Mount Jabalcuz (1650m/5413ft), Jaén is the centre of the most important olive growing district in Spain and probably of the world. Hasdrubal, brother-in-law of Hannibal, made it into an impregnable fortress in 200 BC. It was of great strategic importance at the time of the Moors. The Christians recaptured it in 1246 and beat off frequent counter-attacks, on one occasion (the night of 10-11 June 1430) their decision to surrender being reversed, it is said, by the vision of a procession of angels headed by Mary carrying the infant Jesus.

The **Cathedral** took 270 years to build (1532-1802) and has beautiful carved choir stalls, two magnificent façades – the west front (45m/148ft) designed by Pedro de Vandelvira with figures by Pedro Roldán, and the even more beautiful north front with a huge semi-circular arch. Among the cathedral's possessions are pictures and sculptures by José de Mora, Navarrete, Andrés Guzmán, the Roldán brothers, Jacinto Higueras and one attributed to Titian, an image of the Virgin carried by Bishop Gonzalo de Zúñiga when leading his troops against the Moors and – pride of the cathedral – the *santo rostro*, or holy face, imprinted on a napkin claimed to have been used by St Veronica to wipe the brow of Christ.

Of the churches see: the **Sagrario** (near

the cathedral), 18th-century, designed by Ventura Rodríguez; **San Ildefonso** with retable by *La Roldana* depicting the intervention of the Virgin on the night of 10-11 June 1430; **Mary Magdalene**, oldest church in the town; **San Andrés** with a magnificent wrought-iron screen by Bartolomé of Jaén; **San Bartolomé**, formerly a mosque. Other places to visit: the **Lord Lieutenant's Palace** (*Palacio del Condestable*), built in the 15th century by Moorish craftsmen from Granada; **St Catharine's Castle** (*Castillo de Santa Catalina*), originally Moorish, enlarged by King Ferdinand the Saint; the **Fine Arts Museum** (*Museo de Bellas Artes*) and the **Archaeological Museum** (*Museo Arqueológico*) containing Iberian objects including the famous 'Iberian bull'.

Jerez de la Frontera   M5

Cádiz (pop. 176,200) Centre of the sherry industry, a town of palaces, towers, old walls, innumerable churches and streets shaded by orange and palm trees, Jerez has a pleasant main square with a statue by Benlliure of General Primo de Rivera (1870-1930) who was born at Cádiz. Of the churches see: **St Michael** (*San Miguel*), 15th- to 16th-century, containing a painting by Zurbarán and an altar-piece by Juan Martínez Montañés and José de Arce; the 16th-century **St James** (*Santiago*) with its 18th-century clock tower: **St John** (*San Juan*) in which leaders of the Christian forces wrote a message in their own blood appealing for assistance against the besieging Moors; the main church of the town **La Colegiata**, 1695 to mid-18th-century; and, 4km/2mi outside the town, the 15th-century **Carthusian Monastery** (*La Cartuja*) with its cloisters bordered by the monks' cells.

Linares   F15

Jaén (pop. 54,800) Here the sad-faced, long-nosed *Manolete*, whom every woman in Spain wanted to mother, one of the greatest matadors of all time, was fatally gored in 1947, plunging the country into a week of national mourning. And at nearby Cástulo, Himilce, the lovely wife of Hannibal, was born about 200 BC. See the **Archaeological Museum** (*Museo Arqueológico*), **St Mary's Church** (*Iglesia de Santa María*), the **Old Mint** (*Casa de la Moneda*) and the **Palace of the Marquis of Linares** (*Palacio del Marqués de Linares*).

Loja   K13

Granada (pop. 19,500) Famous for biscuits known as *roscos*, Loja has a **Moorish fortress** (*alcazaba*) built 895 and now in ruins; the early 16th-century **St Gabriel's Church** (*Iglesia de San Gabriel*)

whose dome and doorway are attributed to Diego de Siloé; the **Sanctuary of Our Lady of Charity** (*Santuario de Nuestra Señora de la Caridad*) containing a sculpture of Christ by Alonso Cano; and an impressive waterfall on the River Genil known as the Loja Inferno (*los Infiernos de Loja*).

Málaga   M12

Málaga (pop. 503,300) City of flowers, centre of the Costa del Sol, Málaga was founded by the Phoenicians, occupied by the Moors for 776 years and recaptured by the Catholic Monarchs after a gruesome, two-year siege in 1487. It has a seaport and an airport.

The **Cathedral** was begun in 1528, consecrated in 1588. From its tower (74m/243ft) there is a grandstand view of the town. The cathedral has 15 side chapels, 25 altars, two 18th-century organs (whose builder, Julián de la Orden, lived in the tower so as not to be separated from his masterpieces and there died) and choir stalls exquisitely carved by Pedro de Mena. The ambulatory (*la girola*) has frescoes by Arbasia. In various parts of the cathedral are paintings or sculptures by Ribera, Alonso Cano, Zurbarán, Coello, Van Dyck and Morales. Adjoining the cathedral is the parochial church of **El Sagrario** (1714) possessing a 16th-century reredos by either Berruguete or Balmaseda.

See also: the **Church of St Peter** (*Iglesia de San Pedro*) which has a figure of Christ by Benlliure; the **Church of San Lázaro**, once a leper house and with a crypt decorated by the inmates; the **Church of the Martyrs** (*Iglesia de los Mártires*) containing a crucifix sculpted by the gipsy Juan Vargas; and the **Church of St James** (*Iglesia de Santiago*) with 16th-century tower, tiled dome and 18th-century altarpiece; the **Church of St Mary of the Victory** (*Iglesia de Santa María de la Victoria*) containing a *mater dolorosa* by Pedro de Mena and ironwork said to have been forged from Moorish cannons.

The **Bishop's Palace**, mid-18th-century, is one of the most beautiful buildings in **Málaga**. The **Alcazaba**, built by the Moors in the 11th century as a palace-fortress, still contains many features of superb Moorish workmanship and houses the **Archaeological Museum** (*Museo Arqueológico*). The **Fine Arts Museum** (*Museo de Bellas Artes*) has paintings by Zurbarán, Ribera, Murillo, Morales, Herrera and some early sketches by the locally-born Picasso.

Marbella   N10

Málaga (pop. 67,800) With an important

iron and steel industry, the ruins of a Moorish wall and a 15th-century town hall, Marbella has now become one of the most popular resorts on the Costa del Sol.

Martos   H14
Jaén (pop. 21,700) Spain's biggest refiner of olive oil, Martos is built on the slopes of the rocky hill on which the Carvajal brothers, before being thrown to their death by order of Ferdinand IV (1295-1312), prophesied retribution by God within 30 days. In fact Ferdinand died within that time, here in Martos. See the 13th-century **St Mary's Church** (*Iglesia de Santa María*).

Medina Sidonia   N6
Cádiz (pop. 16,200) A picturesque town on a mountain slope with the ruins of a castle, this was the home of the powerful Dukes of Medina Sidonia, one of whom commanded the Spanish Armada. It was also the birthplace of Admiral Cervera (1839-1909) whose fleet was destroyed in a few hours on 3 July 1898 off Santiago, Cuba, by Admiral Sampson during the Spanish-American war. In the **Church of St Mary the Crowned** (*Iglesia de Santa María Coronada*) is a magnificent altarpiece. See in the district the prehistoric cave **la Cueva del Tajo de las Figuras**.

Moguer   J2
Huelva (pop. 10,000) There is a museum dedicated to Juan Ramón Jiménez, winner of the Nobel prize for poetry. The 16th-century **Church of Our Lady of the Pomegranate** (*Iglesia de Nuestra Señora de la Granada*) contains a painting by Murillo and a sculpture by Alonso Cano and **St Clare's Convent** contains vestments embroidered by Queen Isabel the Catholic.

Montilla   H11
Córdoba (pop. 21,400) Famous for its wine, Montilla has the ruins of a castle where Gonzalo Fernández, the *Gran Capitán*, loyal general of the Catholic Monarchs, was born; the **House and Museum of the Inca Garcilaso de la Vega** where the celebrated Peruvian writer lived for 30 years; the churches of **Santa María** (1525) with a fine *bas relief* in wood; **San Francisco Solano** containing a painting by Murillo and images attributed to Martínez Montañés and Juan de Mesa; and **Nuestra Señora del Carmen** containing some fine carvings.

Motril   M15
Granada (pop. 39,800) There is a cane and beet sugar refinery, the ruins of a **Moorish Castle** and walls, a **Moorish Bath** (*el Bañuelo*) and several churches including that of **Nuestra Señora de la Cabeza** built on the site of a palace which housed the harem of the Moorish kings.

Nerja, Caves of   M14
Málaga Situated 5km/3mi from the village of Nerja on the Costa del Sol, these were discovered 1959 and are now visited by 150,000 people each year. Several huge galleries contain Palaeolithic paintings (15-18,000 years BC), Neolithic implements (1500-3000 years BC), bracelets and human remains.

Niebla   I3
Huelva (pop. 4000) Surrounded by a 3km/2mi wall with 46 towers and four gateways. The **Church of St Mary of the Pomegranate** (*Iglesia de Nuestra Señora de la Granada*) has a 12th-century tower, Roman and Moorish capitals and a 2nd-century Christian sarcophagus. There is a small **Museum** founded by the British archaeologist, Mrs E. M. Whishaw.

Osuna   J9
Sevilla (pop. 15,700) The town centre (officially denominated a national monument) has attractive houses with heavy wooden doors, artistic wrought iron grilles and colourful patios. In the 16th-century **Collegiate Church** (*la Colegiata*) are paintings by Ribera, Morales and Giordano and an image of the Virgin by Alonso Cano. See also the sepulchre of the Dukes of Osuna, since the 16th century one of Spain's top noble families.

Palos de la Frontera   J2
Huelva (pop. 5900) From this little port Columbus set sail on his first voyage of discovery in 1492. He enrolled the crew of his three caravels in front of the then-modern **St George's Church** (*Iglesia de San Jorge*). Nearby is **La Fontanilla**, the Roman well from which he drew water for the voyage. 3km/2mi away is the **Monastery of La Rábida** (open to public) in which Columbus sought the help of Friar Juan Pérez to obtain Queen Isabel's support for his venture.

Puerto de Santa María   M5
Cádiz (pop. 57,000) Salt and wine are produced and shipped across the bay to the port of Cádiz. It has a 13th-century **castle** (*Castillo de San Marcos*) still in good condition and containing a memorial tablet to two local men who accompanied Columbus; a **Parish Church** built on the orders of King Alfonso the Learned (1252-84) after he had reconquered the town from the Moors; the Franciscan **Monastery of St Mary of the Victory**, built

in the early 16th century at the expense of the Dukes of Medinaceli but in the 19th century used as a prison; and many fine houses and palaces, some now in ruins.

Ronda   M9

Málaga (pop. 21,400) Famous for the huge gorge (*el tajo*), varying in depth from 190 to 300m/623 to 984ft, which divides the town in two. On the northern side is the *Mercadillo*, the more modern town built since the reconquest. On the south is the fascinating town of tortuous alleys and fine old houses inherited from the Moors.

The **Casa del Rey Moro** (House of the Moorish King) belonged to Abulmelek, Moorish king of Ronda and Algeciras, and has 365 steps leading to the bottom of the gorge. The **Casa del Gigante** (House of the Giant) was the residence of another Moorish king, Aboruelic, as was the **Palace of Mondragón**, a beautiful building later owned by Ferdinand and Isabel. The **Cathedral** (*Catedral de Santa María la Mayor*) was built 1485-1500 by order of Ferdinand and Isabel and reconstructed in the 16th and 17th centuries. The **Church of the Holy Ghost** (*Parroquia del Espíritu Santo*) was originally a mosque. The **Church of St Mary of the Incarnation** (*Santa María de la Encarnación*), modelled on Málaga cathedral, still has a Moorish minaret. There are also the ruins of the Moorish fort, the **Alcazaba**. 12km/7mi away is **Ronda la Vieja** where in 49 BC Caesar defeated Pompey, who is supposed to have hidden in the nearby cave **la Cueva de Pompeyo**. See also the archaeologically important cave, **La Cueva de la Pileta** (26km/16mi W. of Ronda), with prehistoric wall paintings.

San Lúcar de Barrameda   L4

Cádiz (pop. 48,500) At the mouth of the River Guadalquivir, this town is famous for its dry sherry-type wine *manzanilla*. From its port Columbus set sail on his third voyage (1498) and Magellan on his voyage of discovery to the Philippines (1519). After Magellan's death there Elcano took command and returned home after completing the first ever circumnavigation of the globe. Of the original five caravels, only one returned, of the original 265 sailors only 17, nearly all ill. San Lúcar has several lovely palaces (including that of the Dukes of Medina Sidonia) and the 14th-century **Church of Our Lady of Hope** (*Iglesia de Nuestra Señora de la O*).

San Roque   O8

Cádiz (pop. 20,600) This pretty little town on a hilltop overlooking the Bay of Gibraltar was the refuge of those who left the Rock when Britain captured it in 1704. In the 17th-century **Church of Our Lady Crowned** (*Iglesia de Nuestra Señora Coronada*) are the tombs of the Spanish heroes who died in attempts to retake the fortress from the British.

Santafé   K14

Granada (pop. 10,900) Its name means 'Holy Faith', and it was built in 1491 by the Catholic Monarchs to give more substantial accommodation to their troops besieging Granada after their tents had been set on fire. The four original town gates, restored in the 18th century, still remain.

Sevilla   J6

Sevilla (pop. 653,800) On the River Guadalquivir, no more than 8m/26ft above sea level, the only inland port in Spain, a university town, seat of a bishopric, spiritual home of bullfighting and a very lovely city, Sevilla is famous for pottery, tiles, wrought ironwork, jewellery, ladies' fans, bullfighters' suits, olives and bitter oranges. Its Royal Tobacco Factory (now a college) was the setting for Bizet's *Carmen*. Its *Barrio de Santa Cruz*, a district of cool alleyways, shady patios and wrought-iron gates, is the most heavenly place in Spain.

Sevilla was important under the Romans (Julius Caesar was here in person in 49BC) and in Moorish times was defended from its 166 towers. For many years after 1492 Sevilla was the only port allowed to trade with the newly-discovered Americas, a privilege it lost to Cádiz in 1717.

The 15th-century **Cathedral**, biggest in Spain and third biggest (after St Peter's, Rome, and St Paul's, London) in the world, occupies an area of two acres (110 by 70m/361 by 230ft). When the building was projected the dean is quoted as having said: 'Let us build a church so big that those who see it will think us mad.' It is the only cathedral in the world where dances (*las Seises*, on 8 Dec., by young boys in medieval dress in honour of the Virgin's Immaculate Conception) are performed before the high altar. It has five naves, nine superb doorways and 81 stained-glass windows. Nevertheless its interior is gloomy. There are tombs of Christopher Columbus and his son, of King Ferdinand the Saint (1217-52) and his queen, and of King Alfonso the Learned (1252-84); paintings by Murillo, Zurbarán, Jordaens, Goya, Morales, Titian, Van Dyck, Van der Weyden. The reredos (21 by 14m/69 by 46ft) is the biggest in the world. The Gate of Forgiveness (*Puerta del Perdón*) and the Court of the Orange Trees (*Patio de los Naranjos*) were part of the Moorish mosque on the same site. So was the famous **Giralda tower**, built 1184-98 on Roman foundations and in 1578 increased in height to 105m/344ft, fitted with a peal of bells and crowned with a statue of Faith (4m/13ft high, weight 1¼ tons) which rotates with the slightest breeze and thus explains its name *Giralda* (*girar*, to rotate).

The 17th-century **Hospital of Charity** (*Hospital de la Caridad*) is said to have been founded by Miguel de Mañara, the original *Don Juan*, who composed his own epitaph: 'Here lie the bones and ashes of the wickedest man who inhabited this earth'. It has paintings by Valdés Leal, Murillo, Titian and others. The **Torre del Oro**, or golden tower, on the banks of the river, once faced with gold-coloured tiles, was built as a fortress in 1226 by the Moorish governor Abu-el-Ola and used as a gaol in the reign of Pedro the Cruel (1350-69). It is now the **Maritime Museum**.

The Moorish **Alcazaba**, converted into a palace by Pedro the Cruel, was later used as a residence by King Ferdinand and Queen Isabel. Among its many lovely features, all outstanding examples of Moorish and later architecture: the *Patio de las Doncellas* (Court of the Maidens), the *Patio de las Muñecas* (Court of the Dolls), the *Sala de los Embajadores* (Hall of the Ambassadors), the *Dormitorio de los Reyes Moros* (Sleeping Quarters of the Moorish Kings) and the lovely gardens.

Other things to see in Sevilla: the **Casa de Pilatos**, supposed to be a copy of the house of the Pontius Pilates in Jerusalem; the 16th-century **Casa Lonja**, designed by Herrera and housing the **Archivo de Índias**, the world's most valuable collection of documents on Spanish America; the **Fine Arts Museum** (*Museo de Bellas Artes*) in the old Convent of Mercy, containing paintings by Zurbarán, Murillo, El Greco, sculptures by Juan de Mesa and Alonso Cano and engravings by Teniers and Selma; the **Archaeological Museum** (*Museo Arqueológico*) in the lovely **Park of María Luisa** (site of the Hispano-American exhibition of 1928) with its five rooms devoted to Roman finds at Itálica (8km/5mi away and worth visiting); the **Palace of the Dukes of Alba** also known as *Las Casas de las Dueñas* with its many charming patios; the **Church of St Anne** (*Iglesia de Santa Ana*), built in 1280 in the Triana district, the oldest parish church in Sevilla; the **Church of the Macarena**, modern· and containing the famous image of the Macarena attributed to *La Roldana*; and the well-known *Calle de las Sierpes*, the lovely, winding shopping street for pedestrians only.

Tarifa   P7

Cádiz (pop. 15,200) Morocco is 13km/8mi away across the water. This is where the Moorish invasion started in 711 and the whole town is still Moorish in character. In addition to towers, gates and old walls, there are the remains of the **Alcazaba**, the historic castle which Alonso Pérez de Guzmán (Guzmán the Good, 1256-1309) refused to surrender, his defiance meaning death to his nine-year-old son, held hostage by the besiegers. 12km/7mi away are the Roman ruins of *Bolonia*, with walls, capitol, amphitheatre and aqueduct.

Torremolinos   M11

Málaga (pop. 5000) An excellent beach has helped Torremolinos to become one of the major resorts of the Costa del Sol.

Úbeda   F16

Jaén (pop. 28,700) In the middle of the fertile plain of Guadalimar, Úbeda is full of ancient buildings too numerous to mention. Among them: the 16th-century **Chapel of the Saviour** (*Sacra Capilla del Salvador*), designed by Diego de Siloé, built and ornamented by Andrés de Vandelvira, and adjoining it the 16th-century **Palacio del Condestable** now a *parador*; the 16th-century **Palace of the Chains** (*Palacio de las Cadenas*), built by Vandelvira and now the town hall and, facing it, the **Church of Santa María de los Reales Alcázares**, oldest church in the town, built over a mosque and still having the small Moorish doorway through which King Ferdinand III entered on the day of liberation 1234; the **Church of St Paul** (*Iglesia de San Pablo*) one of the most beautiful examples of Gothic architecture in Andalucía; **St James's Hospital** (*Hospital de Santiago*), built by Vandelvira and resembling the Escorial.

Utrera   J6

Sevilla (pop. 37,900) Famous for its olive oil, cotton and fighting bulls, Utrera has a magnificent 14th-century **Moorish castle**; a town wall with 34 towers; the **Palace of the Cuadra Family** (*Palacio de los Cuadra*) now the town hall; the 15th-century **Church of the Assumption** (*Iglesia de la Asunción*), with interesting doorway, tower, choir stalls; the 15th-century **Church of St James** (*Iglesia de Santiago*) with tiled exterior, lovely doorway, image of St Joseph attributed to *La Roldana* and a crypt in which, it is said, corpses mummify themselves naturally; and the **Monastery of St Francis of Assisi** (*San Francisco de Asís*) before whose image of the Virgin of Truth the town council kneel each 15 Aug. to perpetuate a tradition dating back to 1607.

Vejer de la Frontera   O6

Cádiz (pop. 13,500) On 21 Oct. 1805 the
inhabitants of this typically lovely Andalusian town of white-washed houses certainly heard and probably saw the tremendous
broadside (which itself dismounted 20
guns and killed or wounded 400 men) fired
from the 100 guns of Nelson's *Victory*
against the French admiral Villeneuve's
Bucentaire to open the Battle of Trafalgar.
Of the 38 ships in the Franco-Spanish fleet
19 were captured but only four safely
reached harbour in Gibraltar, along with
Victory bearing the body of Nelson (killed
by a musket wound in the chest) pickled in
a barrel of brandy lashed to the mainmast,
for onward shipment to London and
burial in St Paul's.

Vélez Málaga   M13

Málaga (pop. 41,800) Thought to have
been the Phoenician settlement *Menaka*
of 600 years BC, it is claimed its first
church was founded by the Apostle James
when he came to Spain about AD 36. It
has a **Moorish Castle** (*Alcázar*), the
Church of Our Lady of the Incarnation
(*Iglesia de Nuestra Señora de la Encarnación*), until 1487 a mosque; and the **Palace
of Veniel**, once official residence of the
lord-lieutenant.

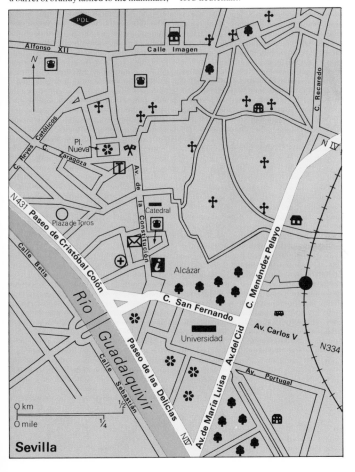

Sevilla

MURCIA

Most Spanish rivers have water in them only when it rains. Then they have too much and sometimes whole villages and their occupants are washed away. A more than typical area where since time immemorial man has battled against alternate drought and inundation is this southeastern region of Murcia. Water, which the rest of Europe takes for granted, has always here been man's overriding preoccupation, deciding where he makes his home, how he lives and even whether he lives at all.

Above everything it decides what he grows. In the mountains, in many areas, that often means nothing, or in some places, trees; in the sandy, semi-desert areas (as the Carthaginians discovered 2500 years ago and founded matting industries to use it) esparto grass.

But the southern part enjoys the inestimable benefit of a river, the 340km/211mi Segura, with water in it all the time. Even that has been a mixed blessing, periodical torrential rains often bringing disaster. There was enormous devastation in 1879. In 1561 1000 houses and 1000 people were swept away and water reached the top of the pulpit in Murcia cathedral. Whenever danger threatened, warnings were sounded on huge seashell 'horns' known as *caracolas*. Every time the river flooded – until recently – water sufficient for the whole population for months rushed uselessly into the sea. Now things are different. Enormous reservoirs controlled by dams and sluices (the biggest, at El Cenajo, built in 1960, 86m/282ft high and holding back 480 million cubic metres) now feed thousands of miles of irrigation channels and make the *huerta* fertile, prosperous and safe to live in.

This is nowadays where most of Spain's fresh, canned or dried apricots come from, most of its lemons and many of its tomatoes and *pimentón*, ground from the red peppers one sees laid out in colourful patches to dry in the autumn sun.

Along this coast the fishermen's boats are fitted with acetylene lamps to attract the fish to the surface at night and into the nets. And at Escombreras, also on the coast, is Spain's only oil refinery, built to deal with crudes from North Africa and the Middle East and producing also chemicals, lubricants, butane and propane gas and fertilizers.

Local fiestas Week following Easter Sunday: Murcia. Tuesday: *Bando de la Huerta* or farm workers' procession during which humorous *bandos* making fun of official mayoral *bandos* or

announcements are read out. Folk dancing. Kiosks selling local produce. Thursday: Battle of flowers. Music. Majorettes. Saturday: Night festival. Thousands of presents thrown to crowds. Ends with fireworks and 'burying of the sardine'. May 2-5: Caravaca (Murcia). Mock battles between Moors and Christians. Horse race of 'knights of the wine'. Blessing of wine, water and flowers. July 16: San Pedro del Pinatar (Murcia). Statue of Virgin carried through streets by fishermen, then procession of fishing boats, solemn mass and return.

Caravaca   K3
Murcia (pop. 20,200) Despite its name (which means cowface) Caravaca is a very pleasant town. It is almost completely surrounded by the biggest apricot plantation in Spain, so that the whole area is a sea of blossom in spring and a mountain of fruit at the end of May. Overlooking the town are the remains of a castle in which, in 1232, the captured Moorish king Muley Acebutey was converted to Christianity when the holy cross of Jerusalem, borne by two angels, suddenly arrived in the middle of mass. The miracle is still celebrated 1-5 May. The 15th-century Church of the Holy Cross (*Iglesia de la Santa Cruz*) is within the castle walls.

Cartagena   M7
Murcia (pop. 172,800) Port, naval base, centre of mining and heavy industry, Cartagena is thought to have been the legendary city of *Mastia* and was colonized in 223 BC by Hannibal's brother-in-law Hasdrubal who named it *Cartago Nuevo* (New Carthage). The town was later (209 BC) brilliantly retaken by the Romans under Publius Cornelius Scipio and became the first of the colonies they established in Spain during their occupation lasting more than six centuries. It was

here, it is claimed, that St James the Apostle landed about AD 36-40 to bring the gospel to Spain (See also **Zaragoza**). From here (13 April 1931) King Alfonso XIII and his English queen, Victoria Eugenia, sailed away to exile. And from here (26 Oct. 1936) the Bank of Spain's controversial gold (51 metric tons) was secretly shipped to Russia for safe keeping and never seen again.

The 17th- to 18th-century **Church of Our Lady of Grace** (*Santa María de Gracia*) contains statues by Salzillo of the three sons and a daughter of the remarkable 6th-century Severiano family, all four of whom became saints. Also worth seeing: the ruins of the **Old Cathedral** (*Catedral Antigua*) claimed to have been the first Christian church in Spain and destroyed by extremists in the Civil War; the **Torre Ciega** or Roman funeral monument of first century AD; the **Archaeological Museum** (*Museo Arqueológico*) containing the most complete collection of Roman mining equipment in existence; and the early **submarine**, 21m/69ft long, designed for a crew of ten, built by the local engineer Isaac Peral in 1887-8.

The old castle, now a park (*Parque Torres*), affords a fine view of the port and the lovely land-locked bay.

Jumilla   H6

Murcia (pop. 20,000) is famous for one thing - strong wine. While normal table wines contain 11 to 12 degrees of alcohol some of Jumilla's boast of 17, and put it into writing by printing it on the label. Try the red wine known as *Pura Sangre* (Pure Blood) for example. Alas there is nothing in the town to see.

Lorca   M4

Murcia (pop. 60,600) Noted for handwoven textiles, lead mines, pottery and wine, Lorca is a picturesque town of old, escutcheoned houses. It has the remains of a **Moorish castle** (recalling the famous battle between two factions of Moors after which Abelmelek sent the head of Yusuf el Febri to his chief in Córdoba as proof of the completion of his task) and whose *Alfonsina tower* honours King Alfonso the Learned (1252-84), liberator of the town; and the lovely **House of the Guevara Family** (*Casa Solariega de Guevara*).

Mar Menor   M8

Murcia The Mar Menor or 'lesser sea' is a sea lagoon 112 sq km/43sq mi in area and nowhere more than 7m/23ft deep. It lies at the northern end of Murcia's 110km/68mi Mediterranean coastline. It is almost totally enclosed by a 25km/15mi long neck of land varying in width from 250m/275yd to 800m/880yd and known as **La Manga**. On either side are sandy beaches. The

water in the Mar Menor is always several degrees warmer than in the open sea. It is ideal for bathing, sailing, water skiing and windsurfing. The whole area is rapidly developing into a centre of international tourism.

Murcia   K6

Murcia (pop. 288,600) Part old, part modern, centre of the fertile *huerta* watered by the River Segura, Murcia is a place of good restaurants and pretty girls. The pedestrians-only streets of its colourful town centre are lined with attractive shops, bars and pavement cafés. It was important under the Moors who established themselves here in 743 and immediately proceeded to modernize the primitive system of irrigation. They stayed more than 500 years, being finally driven out by James I of Aragón in 1266. Murcia was the birthplace of Juan de la Cierva (1895-1936), inventor of the autogiro, who was killed in an air crash at Croydon, England, where his autogiro was being developed in local workshops.

The **Cathedral** (*Catedral de Santa María*), 1394-1465, whose 92m/302ft high tower is a landmark - 'it rises in compartments, like a telescope', wrote the 19th-century traveller Richard Ford - has a fine west front by Jaime Bort, three doorways (the Gate of the Chains, the Gate of the Sinners and the Gate of the Apostles) and the tombs of two of the four Cartagena saints. See also **St Clare's Convent** (*Convento de Santa Clara*), 1284, containing Moorish plasterwork; the **Diocesan Museum** (*Museo Diocesano*) containing an immensely valuable solid silver monstrance, Roman sarcophagi and sculptures by Salzillo; **the Archaeological Museum** (*Museo Arqueológico*) in the lovely House of Culture (*Casa de la Cultura*); the **Fine Arts Museum** (*Museo de Bellas Artes*) with its paintings by Ribera, Sorolla, Ribalta and others; the paintings of Zurbarán and Giordano in the **County Hall** (*Diputación Provincial*) and the **Salzillo Museum** housed in the circular church of Our Father Jesus (*Nuestro Padre Jesús*) and devoted to the work of the celebrated sculptor Francisco Salzillo (1707-83), born in Murcia to a Spanish father and an Italian mother. More of his work can be seen in the churches of **St Bartholomew** (*San Bartolomé*), **St Nicholas** (*San Nicolás*), in which are also works by Alonso Cano and Pedro de Mena; and **St Michael** (*San Miguel*). 6km/4mi from Murcia is the famous **Moorish waterwheel** *la Rueda de la Ñora*.

BALEARES

This group of islands lying 90 to 200km/56 to 124mi off Spain's Mediterranean coast, with its beaches, clear blue seas, reliable summers and spring-like winters, night-life and yachting, is undoubtedly the most popular holiday area in Europe.

The largest of the islands is Mallorca, which measures 100 by 66km/62 by 41mi, has 200km/124mi of coastline with no fewer than 100 beaches and inlets and claims to have the highest concentration of hotels in the world. It is the only Balearic island to have mountains (just as Ibiza is the only island to have a river), its highest peak, Major de Torrelles, rising to 1445m/4741ft. It has many caves, some of them (see **Drach** and **Artá**) major tourist attractions.

Its language is *malloquín*, which is to all intents and purposes Catalan. Its greatest scholar, Ramón Llull (c1235-1315), who firmly believed in the existence of another continent 200 years before Columbus finally discovered it and whose first book contained a million words, was one of the first authors to write in Catalan. Another famous son, Juniper Serra (1713-84) who was born at Petra (where you can see his birthplace, now a museum to his memory) set up Christian missions in what are today the great cities of Monterrey, San Francisco, Los Angeles and San Diego.

Hannibal, they say, though nobody knows for sure, was born on the little island of Conejera, off Mallorca's south coast. Certainly the Carthaginians were occupying the Balearics 400 years before his birth in 247 BC and his famous regiment of stone-slingers which the Romans feared is known to have been composed of Mallorcan men.

Chopin (see **Valldemosa**) spent an unhappy winter in Mallorca in an abandoned monastery 'whose cloisters were full of ghosts and horrors for him', wrote George Sand, but where he nevertheless 'wrote the loveliest of those brief works which he so modestly called preludes'. (Many people say they can recognize the boom of the local church clock in Prelude Opus 28 number 2.)

Mallorca, like all the Balearic Islands, was occupied by the Moors from the 8th century until it was retaken in 1229 by the 21-year-old James I the Conqueror, king of Aragón and Cataluña. His invasion fleet of 150 transports and carrying 6500 men set out from Salou and took the city of Palma after a three and a half month siege.

The second largest island, Menorca, cooler and windier than Mallorca though still hot enough and no less beautiful, is of great interest to archaeologists because of its prehistoric *talayots*, or low, stone-built conical towers, and its *navetes*, again stone-built and in the form of an upturned boat, both of which were probably built in Bronze Age times as sepulchres. There are also numerous *taulas*, or tables, formed of one massive horizontal stone balanced on a similar vertical one and thought to be funeral monuments.

Menorca was for a period of 68 years a British possession. It was first occupied by Britain in 1711 during the War of Spanish Succession, but lost to the French in 1756 after a siege of 70 days (which Vice-Admiral Byng failed to raise and was thus executed for neglect of duty, and '*pour encourager les autres*' according to Voltaire). It was again ceded to Britain in 1763 but in 1782 the depleted garrison of 700 under General Murray surrendered to 12,000 French and Spaniards under De Crillon. In 1798 it was again captured by the British but in 1802 ceded back to Spain. From this long British domination of their island the Menorcans have inherited sash windows (unknown elsewhere in Spain), tall house façades without balconies, the rocking chair and a gin distillery.

Local fiestas January 16-17: La Puebla (Mallorca). Traditional songs, dances. Bonfires in the streets. Blessing of horses and donkeys on 17th (St Anthony). June 23-24: Ciudadela (Menorca). Pilgrimage to local hermitage. 24th Jousting on horseback. July (Sunday following 28th): Palma de Mallorca. Choral procession commemorating entry of St Catherine Thomas. Early August: Eivissa (Ibiza). Processions. Sailing regatta. Battle of flowers. Fireworks. Regional dancing. Bullfights. Sept 7-9: Mahón (Menorca). Folk dancing. Regatta. Horse racing. Fireworks.

Artá, Caves of   D17

Mallorca The caves, formed by the action of the sea, are extraordinary for their beauty and loftiness. There are several 'halls' – the 'vestibule' with roof blackened by the candles of last century's visitors (today there is electric light) – and those of the 'Queen of the Columns', the 'Inferno' and the 'Flags'.

Eivissa   H9

Baleares (pop. 25,500) This sparklingly picturesque capital of the island of Ibiza was founded by the Phoenicians about 650 BC. It is blessed with a benevolent climate and washed by the bluest of seas. It has a seaport and an airport. The wall that surrounds the *D'Alt Vila* or old town on the hill, built 1554-85 on Moorish foundations, has seven towers and three gates and is the only wall of its type still intact in Europe. Its district of *la Peña* is a maze of streets and white-washed houses.

The **cathedral**, built in the 13th to 14th centuries on the site of former Roman and Moorish temples, badly restored in the 17th century, has a valuable 14th-century monstrance in silver-gilt and enamel. The 16th-century **Church of Santo Domingo** has an interesting roof and, in the side chapel of Our Lady of the Rosary, a much-admired reredos. The **Archaeological Museum** (*Museo Arqueológico*) contains the world's finest collection of Punic or Carthaginian art, mostly discovered on the local hill known as *Puig des Molins*, on which is an important 7th-century BC necropolis with more than 3000 burial chambers cut out of the rock. The **Ethnic Museum** (*Museo Étnico*) contains costumes, firearms and other objects relating to the history of Ibiza.

Formentera   I9
Baleares (pop. 3500) The name means the Isle of Wheat (a true name in Roman times). This is the fourth largest (measuring 15 by 8km/9 by 5mi) of the Balearic Islands. Near its small port, *La Sabina*, are some very ancient salt pans producing 20,000 tons of salt a year. The island is developing as a holiday resort.

Mahón   C20
Baleares (pop. 22,900) Displacing Ciutadella as capital of Menorca during the British occupation in the 18th century, Mahón has one of the best natural ports in the Mediterranean, guarded by the fort which the British named Georgetown and the Spaniards renamed Villacarlos (Charlestown) after theirs.

Mahón has a proprietorial interest in *mahonesa* which the French are accused of stealing and calling mayonnaise, and also in David Glasgow Farragut (1801-70) because his parents were Menorcans. He entered the US navy at the age of nine and eventually became its first admiral.

Manacor   E16
Mallorca (pop. 24,200) Famous for artificial pearls and (11km/7mi distant) the **Caves of Drach** with rock formations in fantastic shapes in a series of interconnected 'halls' covering 2km/1mi and with the largest subterranean lake in the world (200m/656ft long) on which concerts of classical music are given.

Palma de Mallorca   E14
Baleares (pop. 304,400) Standing in the centre of a 20km/12mi bay with an important harbour and a fine yacht basin,

Palma is one of the most popular tourist resorts in Europe. It has 1500 hotels and first class pensions but no adequate beach of its own (though there are good beaches within a few km to east and west).

The **Cathedral** (*la Seo*) started in 1230 after the town's liberation from the Moors by James I of Cataluña and Aragón, was not completed until early 17th century. It has a magnificent rose window (11m/36ft in diameter and claimed to be the largest in the world) three naves, the central one (1380) 43m/141ft high and formed by 14 slender columns. In the cathedral are the bodies of kings James II and James III and of Bishop Giles Muñoz who as Clement VIII was one of the anti-popes or rival popes set up in Geneva in the 14th century. The **Old Exchange** (*la Lonja*), designed by Guillermo Sagrera and built in the first half of the 15th century, has four main turrets, a very fine doorway and three naves and now houses the **Provincial Museum** containing 15th- and 16th-century retables and paintings by Spanish and Italian masters. The nearby 17th-century **Consulado de Mar**, formerly the tribunal of commerce, has an attractive Renaissance loggia and is now used as a **Maritime Museum**.

Also of interest in Palma: the **Bishop's Palace**, early 17th-century and now the Diocesan Museum; the **Almudaina Palace**, former residence of the Moorish kings, though rebuilding in the 14th and 16th centuries obliterated most of the Moorish workmanship; and in the palace courtyard the **Chapel of Santa Ana** with a romanesque doorway and an interesting altar-piece; **Bellver Castle**, 14th-century, moated and circular in form and with a majestic tower of homage, a prison until 1915 (the statesman Jovellanos was incarcerated there, and in 1808 Napoleonic officer-prisoners), stands on high ground overlooking the town and now houses the **Archaeological Museum**; the **Arab Baths** (*Baños Árabes*), Palma's only Moorish building in its original state; the **Church of Santa Eulalia**, built in the same style as the cathedral and containing an impressive altar-piece; the **Church of St Francis of Assisi**, 13th-century with 17th-century main doorway and containing the tomb of Ramón Llull (c.1235-1315), the Mallorca-born philosopher who introduced the study of oriental languages to Oxford, Paris and other seats of learning; and many interesting houses in the old town.

Valldemosa   D14

Baleares (pop. 1200) A lovely Mallorcan village that inspired the poet Rubén Darío and painters Rusiñol, Miró and Vázquez Díaz. At the Carthusian Monastery (*La Cartuja*), where Jovellanos was held prisoner, in whose church Goya's brother-in-law Manuel Bayeu painted the frescoes, Chopin spent the winter of 1838-9 with his friend George Sand. Here he wrote most of his preludes, two polonaises, the second *Ballade in F Major* (Opus 38), the *Sonata in B Flat Minor* (Opus 35) and possibly the *Funeral March*, the saddest piece of music he ever wrote and reflecting the monastic gloom that depressed him so much.

Ciudadela, Menorca

All main entries are printed in heavy type. Map references are also printed in heavy type. The map page number precedes the grid reference.